The ATLAS
OF THE EARTH

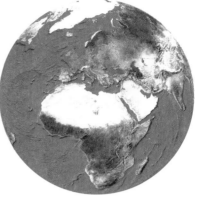

The
ATLAS
OF THE
EARTH

Alexa Stace

Consultant Editor: Dougal Dixon

THE ATLAS OF THE EARTH

Z-Publishing Ltd.
7-11 St. Johns Hill
London SW11 1TN
United Kingdom

This edition published in North America
2002 by Michael Friedman Publishing Group, Inc.
Originally published by Z-Publishing Ltd. © 2001

ISBN 1-58663-344-9
10 9 8 7 6 5 4 3 2 1

The publishers would like to thank
Robert Stacey and Emery Miller of WorldSat International Inc., Mary-Louise Schmid and
Debbie Dodds of NASA (Johnson Space Flight Center), and Rob Bauer of the University of
Colorado at Boulder (Snow and ICE Data Center–Cooperative Institute for Research in
Environmental Sciences), for their help in producing this book.

Printed in Spain

Contents

Introduction

SINCE THE dawn of civilization people have been trying to understand their own world. The earliest maps, produced

by the ancient Greeks, showed the islands and coastlines of the Mediterranean Sea—the limit of known travel for their galleys and sailing ships.

The study of mathematics, astronomy, geology, and the other sciences brought about more and more accurate surveying, and as the world became better known in the Middle Ages, the maps of the Earth became gradually more detailed and more meaningful.

In modern times, the development of air travel enabled us to see, for the first time, our living landscape from above. The shapes of islands, the courses of rivers, the layouts of cities could now be seen directly. It was even possible for astronauts, flying high enough, to detect the actual curvature of the horizon.

Now we live in the Space Age. In the late 1960s, the first manned expeditions to the moon brought us back photographs of our own planet as a sparkling jewel set in the empty, star-studded darkness of infinite space—the entire planet on a single photograph frame.

We can now send satellites into orbit to look down on our own world, with a whole array of cameras, scanners, and sensors. Computers can analyze data and present it in the form of photographs, altered so that the false colors produced can reveal surface features invisible in normal light. As well as showing us just what our world looks like, these techniques have had far-

reaching effects on all kinds of environmental studies, including agriculture, forestry,

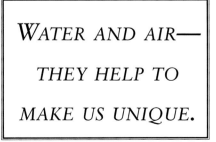

WATER AND AIR— THEY HELP TO MAKE US UNIQUE.

The photographs taken from space and published in this book have either come from satellites, such as Landsat, or have been taken by astronauts from a space shuttle.

Space imaging has come a long way since John Glenn first snapped a few pictures from his capsule on February 20, 1962. Nowadays it is possible to photograph objects less than 3 feet (1 m) wide from near space, "see" under desert sands, and find long-lost rivers.

Conventional photography

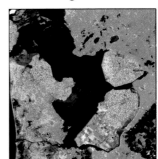

False-color image

LANDSAT

PICTURES IN 0s AND 1s

When a signal is beamed down from a satellite to a satellite dish it is then conveyed as digital data along special telephone lines to a computer.

Once captured and "cleaned up" the data can be made available to the public in a number of ways, as either natural or false-color images.

AROUND THE EARTH IN 90 MINUTES

The space shuttle—actually three different crafts—has carried cameras since the early missions in the 1980s. The photography is usually handheld, using conventional cameras. Sometimes special infrared film is used.

SPACE SHUTTLE

0010011011
1000111011
0101111011
1011001101

urban planning, and the location of mineral and water resources.

Diagrams in textbooks have always been valuable in presenting the theory behind geographic features. Now we can back up those diagrams with images from space. We can see just how a river follows its course from the mountains to the sea; we can see the march of sand dunes across an entire desert; we can see the different kinds of coral produced as an island chain ages. The elegance, the simplicity, the complexity of the Earth's natural processes, and

the human modification of them, can now be seen directly.

We can present a

snapshot album of our own home!

Dougal Dixon,
Consultant Editor

FIRE AND HEAT—
NATURE AT ITS
MOST
SPECTACULAR

PART ONE

A living planet

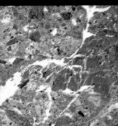

The Earth in action:
how movements in the Earth's crust,
its atmosphere, and even outer space
shape the planet

Earth in space

See also:
- **The air around us** *p. 14*
- **Moving plates** *p. 18*
- **Spreading rifts** *p. 22*
- **Building mountains** *p. 24*

WHERE WE ARE IN SPACE

The nine planets of the solar system are either small and rocky or huge and made of gas. The Earth is the largest of the five known rocky planets, four of which lie close to the sun. It is only one-eighth the diameter of Jupiter, the largest of the gas giants.

9 Pluto

8 Neptune

7 Uranus

6 Saturn

5 Jupiter

4 Mars

3 Earth

2 Venus

1 Mercury

THE SUN is the life-giving force for our planet, and the distance of the Earth from the sun is essential for the continuation of life. The "eco-sphere" is the region around the sun with a suitable temperature to sustain life. Inside the inner boundary would be too hot; outside the outer boundary would be too cold. Earth is at the midpoint, with Venus at the inner edge and Mars at the outer. Nowhere else in the solar system can support life as we know it. Although the moon is a similar distance from the sun, it lacks an atmosphere, so the average temperature is 3°F (-16°C), compared with Earth's 59°F (15°C).

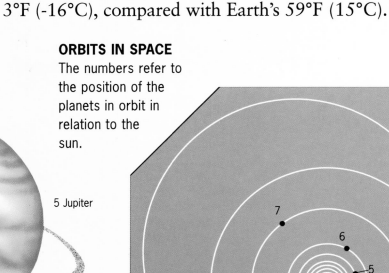

ORBITS IN SPACE

The numbers refer to the position of the planets in orbit in relation to the sun.

EARTHRISE, DECEMBER 22, 1968

Left:

As Apollo VIII *orbited the moon on its prelanding mission, the astronauts took this picture showing our planet rising above the moon's horizon. The moonscape is lit orange by the rays of the sun, which is above the picture.*

ONE THEORY

There are many theories about how Earth came into being. One theory is that one star was hit by another.

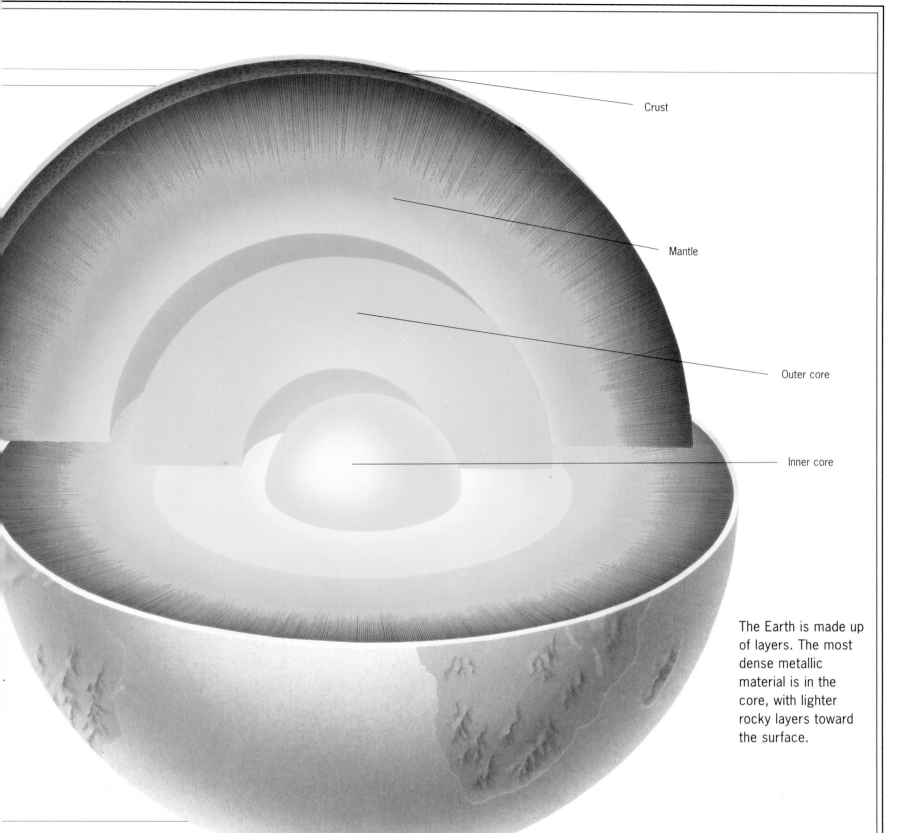

Crust

Mantle

Outer core

Inner core

The Earth is made up of layers. The most dense metallic material is in the core, with lighter rocky layers toward the surface.

After the collision, a chunk of stellar debris was flung off and went into orbit around one of the stars.

The debris cooled and accumulated as the ancestors of the planets—including the Earth. The star became our sun.

INSIDE THE EARTH

We can tell what is inside the Earth by studying the vibrations of earthquake waves. There are two different kinds of vibrations—one makes a back-and-forth movement, and another makes a side-to-side movement. The first can pass through solid and liquid layers, but the second can only pass through solids.

From these studies we know that the center of the Earth—the inner core—is solid. This is surrounded by a liquid outer core. The main bulk of the Earth is the solid rocky mantle, which has a squashy area— the asthenosphere—near the top. The crust, which is the only part we can sample directly, forms a kind of very thin "rind" around the outside.

The air around us

See also:
- **Fallen stars** p. 30
- **Rivers** p. 38
- **...and deltas** p. 42
- **Eroding earth** p. 44

Sun rays strike the atmosphere and are split into various parts.

Below:
This famous image, taken during one of the Apollo *missions in the late 1960s, shows the effect of light splitting into its component parts—refracting—in the atmosphere.*

THE ATMOSPHERE is the outermost "shell" of the Earth's structure. It is composed of a mixture of gases that envelop the whole globe. At first, the atmosphere contained a poisonous mixture of gases such as hydrogen, carbon dioxide, and methane. But as plants evolved they absorbed much of the carbon dioxide and produced oxygen so that gradually the atmosphere became as it is today—a mixture of gases that is able to support animal life.

THE EARTH'S BLANKET

Without the atmosphere, the Earth would be unbearable. The side facing the sun would roast in the heat, while the other side would be freezing. The atmosphere acts like insulation. During the day it filters out most of the harmful rays from the sun, but allows sunlight through. At night, it traps warmth at the Earth's surface and prevents it from radiating into space. But with a different mixture of gases too much heat would be trapped at the surface, producing the "greenhouse effect."

PARTS OF A RAY
1. Most ultraviolet rays are reflected away.
2. Some of the light is reflected back by clouds.
3. Light reaches the surface, but also reflects back.
4. The infrared rays that reach the surface are bounced back.
5. Some of the reflected infrared radiation is trapped in the atmosphere.

Right:
A meteorite burns up as it hits the Earth's atmosphere. Only on rare occasions do they penetrate this shield.

Left:
The atmosphere is colored by pollutants, suspended dust, and other matter. Here the sky has been turned golden red by the dust generated by the 1991 volcanic explosion of Mount Pinatubo in the Philippines. The dust cloud affected a large portion of the Earth's atmosphere, much like the gigantic volcanic explosion of nearby Krakatao in 1883 when ash encircled the whole Earth.

LIFE CYCLES

The Earth is a dynamic system, with something always happening. Nearly all the chemicals that make up the Earth and the living things on it have been here since the Earth was first formed, some 4.6 billion years ago.

When rocks form, they do so from fragments of rocks that existed before. Eventually the new rocks decay or are broken down, and the remains form another generation of rocks.

It is the same in the living systems. All the substances in an animal's or a plant's life cycle are reused over and over again.

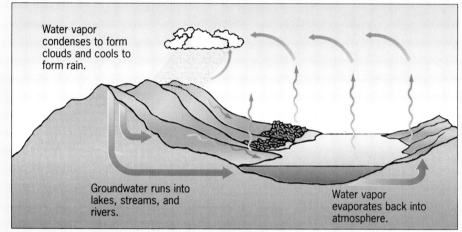

Water vapor condenses to form clouds and cools to form rain.

Groundwater runs into lakes, streams, and rivers.

Water vapor evaporates back into atmosphere.

THE WATER CYCLE

What makes Earth unique is that water is freely available at the surface. It exists in three forms: liquid, solid, and vapor.

Water travels in the oceans and is evaporated by the sun into vapor. The vapor condenses into clouds of droplets, which fall as rain.

The water flows on the surface or through the rocks to emerge as springs. Streams flow downhill, and so water returns eventually to the oceans as rivers.

Along this route water is used by animals, plants, and humans. It is absorbed into their bodies and returned back to the Earth when its work is done.

Oxygen in the atmosphere is breathed in by animals on land. Dissolved in rain, it also oxygenates the sea.

Photosynthesis by plants on land and by marine plants in the sea passes back oxygen into the atmosphere.

CARBON AND OXYGEN CYCLES

Life is based on the workings of organic chemistry. This involves the buildup and breakdown of complex carbon-based molecules.

Oxygen and carbon are constantly moving about in this system.

Carbon is the foundation of all plant and animal life, while oxygen enables the living organisms to breathe.

Carbon dioxide is given off into the atmosphere and breathed in by plants to aid photosynthesis.

Decaying plants and animal waste feed soil.

Earth movements

See also:
- **Moving plates** *p. 18*
- **Volcano!** *p. 20*
- **Spreading rifts** *p. 22*
- **Building mountains** *p. 24*

Underneath the Earth's thin shell lies an enormous, pulsating mass of hot and cool liquid rock on which our continents float. In this computer model, red is hot rock and blue is cool. The flows have been shown separately for clarity.

Hot magma rises up and sometimes escapes through cracks and volcanoes in the Earth's surface.

Cooling magma flows down to the center of the Earth to be reheated.

HUGE SECTIONS, or "plates," of the Earth's hard outer layers produce massive forces as they float on partly molten rock.

The slow movement of these plates—no more than about 5 inches (12.5 cm) a year—affects the shape of the continents. And the forces produced as the plates collide or move apart are responsible, over many millions of years, for the formation of mountains, volcanoes, underwater canyons, and earthquakes.

Volcanoes are formed more dramatically. Molten rock, called "magma," is forced through cracks in the Earth's crust. The magma cools quickly into the solid rock of volcanic mountains.

Cracks on the ocean floor, oozing molten lava, build new sea floor, while the rubbing together of the plates causes earthquakes to take place.

PANGAEA 250M YEARS AGO

HOW THE WORLD HAS CHANGED

The Earth today is very different from what it was like 250 million years ago. Then it was one large landmass, known as Pangaea, with a single ocean—the Tethys Ocean. Gradually, over millions of years, Pangaea split apart in a process known as "continental drift" into the globe that we recognize today.

JURASSIC EARTH 200M YEARS AGO

CRETACEOUS EARTH 150M YEARS AGO

Left:
Active volcanoes are among the most spectacular sights on Earth. This photograph, taken in Hawaii, shows molten rock from inside the Earth's crust oozing out of cracks and slowly cooling.

THE EARTH TODAY

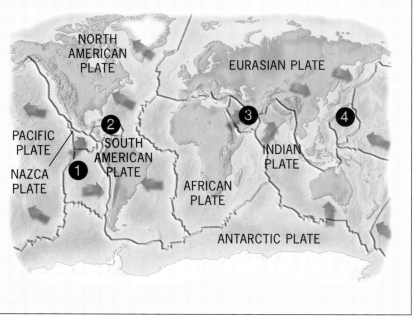

OUR MOVING WORLD

The Earth's upper layer is made up of six major plates and a few smaller ones. Many plates consist of both ocean floor and dry land.

The diagram shows the main plate boundaries, the edges where the Earth's crust is weakest. Most volcanoes and earthquakes occur on these edges.

Key

The main plate boundaries

The direction of movement

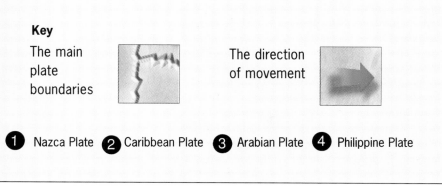

NORTH AMERICAN PLATE

EURASIAN PLATE

PACIFIC PLATE

SOUTH AMERICAN PLATE

INDIAN PLATE

NAZCA PLATE

AFRICAN PLATE

ANTARCTIC PLATE

1 Nazca Plate   **2** Caribbean Plate   **3** Arabian Plate   **4** Philippine Plate

Moving plates

See also:
- **Earth movements** *p. 16*
- **Volcano!** *p. 20*
- **Spreading rifts** *p. 22*
- **Building mountains** *p. 24*

SHALLOW SEA
The North Sea rests on a low, submerged continental shelf. This seabed is slowly expanding east–west with the rest of the Eurasian Plate, creating the rock structures that form the North Sea oil fields.

TWO-WAY STRETCH
The north–south rift valleys of the Rhône and the Rhine Rivers are the result of the European Plate being stretched east–west as the African Plate continues to drag it eastward.

SHRINKING OCEAN
More than 100 million years ago, the mighty Tethys Ocean separated two great continents—the Eurasian Plate and the African Plate. After the collision of the plates some 45 million years ago, all that remains of this ocean are the Mediterranean, the Caspian Sea, and the Black Sea.

IBERIA STRIKES OUT
Spain and Portugal have split away from France, moved south, and swung around. This has opened up the Bay of Biscay and crunched up the land between, forming the Pyrenees Mountains.

MOVING ISLANDS
Plate movement has slowly pulled the islands of Corsica and Sardinia away from the underside of France and Italy and into their present positions.

Above:
Europe, with its valleys, mountains, bays, and islands, is a perfect example of a continent created by tectonics.

THE BARE BONES of all the continents are the result of plate movements, past and present. Colliding plates twist up mountain chains, diverging plates wrench continents apart, and active plate boundaries are the sites of volcanoes and earthquakes.

The shapes of the continents may seem random, but they all represent the legacy of the worldwide movement of the Earth's surface.

SWINGING LANDS

Europe has a solid heart of ancient rock, surrounded by crumpled mountain ranges of younger rock.

These younger rocks have been shaped by continuous plate movement. In the last few 100 million years, the African Plate has moved north, colliding with Europe, squeezing out the ocean between, and throwing up mountain ranges along the edge. Now Africa is moving east, stretching out the fabric of Europe east–west.

These rocks were built up about 300 million years ago.

The Baltic Shield of ancient rocks is partly buried under new rock, which forms Belarus, Poland, and much of Eastern Europe.

These rocks were built up about 200 million years ago.

The Atlas Mountains in Morocco, the Apennines in Italy, the Alps, and the Carpathian Mountains in Eastern Europe have all been twisted into a continuous S-shape as the two continents—Europe and Africa—ground past each other.

These rocks were built up about 50 million years ago and are the youngest in Europe. They are also the most earthquake prone and volcanically active.

The present position of Australia.

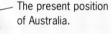

WALTZING MATILDA, WALTZING MATILDA

Australia was originally part of Gondwana, the southern super-continent that also included Antarctica, India, Africa, and South America. Gondwana began to break up about 200 million years ago, splitting into the various continents as we now know them. Australia was the last to move, breaking off from Antarctica about 85 million years ago and drifting northward. It is still moving. Some day it will collide with the mainland of Asia, and vast mountain ranges like the Himalayas will be thrown up in between.

Australia's progress north, as part of Gondwana and then as a single continent, can be plotted by examining the magnetism in rocks formed at certain times.

85 million years ago, Australia split from Antarctica.

Right:
Marsupials like this opossum probably spread from the Americas to Australia via Antarctica at the time when these continents were all joined together.

Volcano!

See also:
- **Earth movements** p. 16
- **Moving plates** p. 18
- **Spreading rifts** p. 22
- **Shake, rattle, and roll** p. 26

Above:
As the space shuttle Endeavor *passed over the Kamchatka Peninsula, just north of Japan, it observed the belching smoke stream out of the Klyuchevskaya volcano. An andesitic volcano, its September 1994 explosion shot smoke and ash 36,949 feet (11,262 m) into the atmosphere. Winds then carried the debris over 640 miles (1,030 km). Air traffic had to fly longer routes to avoid the ash cloud.*

Klyuchevskaya is one of a group of 20 volcanoes along the peninsula, situated on the Pacific "Ring of Fire." They erupt, on average, three to five times each year.

THE GREATEST FORCES on Earth can be unleashed when a volcano erupts—or it could be a small stream of molten magma slowly cooling into rock. Such is the unpredictable nature of volcanic activity. This is why volcanoes are so dangerous.

The most famous eruption occurred in Italy in AD 79, when Mount Vesuvius smothered the Roman towns of Pompeii and Herculaneum in hot ash. In 1883 Krakatao, an island volcano east of Java, blew apart and disappeared overnight, and in 1991 Mount Pinatubo in the Philippines produced the greatest volcanic explosion of that century.

THE TWO TYPES OF VOLCANOES

Cone volcanoes, formed by explosive andesitic magma, are to be found in the Pacific's "Ring of Fire."

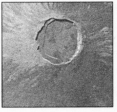

Shield volcanoes are less explosive and have the gently spreading slopes typical of Hawaiian volcanoes.

The shock wave can easily be seen around the volcano's slopes. Within the blast area, all the trees had been felled in the same direction.

WHEN WASHINGTON BLEW ITS TOP

On the morning of May 18, 1980, Mount St. Helens erupted. Its summit collapsed, the sides of the volcano burst outward triggering landslides, and a searingly hot ash cloud shot upward for almost 12 miles (19 km). Within two weeks, this cloud had encircled the Earth.

During its eruption, the volcano ejected 1 cubic mile (4 cu km) of airborne debris and lost 1,300 feet (396 m) of its original height. Sadly, eight geological observers lost their lives after being caught by the blast. The blast was the first volcanic eruption in the continental United States for over 60 years.

The mountain first exploded sideways, bulging outward. The force was the equivalent of a 10 megaton bomb—500 times more powerful than the bomb that destroyed Hiroshima in 1945.

MAY 18, 1980
DURING

The white–hot ash and dust, lubricated by expanding gases—pyroclastic flow—rushed downward at 100 miles per hour (170 kph) and, with the blast, swept away 497 square miles (1,287 sq km) of prime timber.

JUNE, 1980
AFTER

Right:
The aftermath of the cataclysmic explosion and blast wave.

Spreading rifts

See also:
- **Earth movements** *p. 16*
- **Moving plates** *p. 18*
- **Volcano!** *p. 20*
- **Building mountains** *p. 24*

Below:
The western coastline of Africa matches that of South America, from which it split 120 million years ago.

NEW PLATES form as molten rock from the Earth's interior wells up along cracks and solidifies. This usually happens under the sea, producing the ocean ridges. But sometimes it occurs beneath a continent, causing it to split up and break apart. This is what is happening to Africa.

A satellite photograph clearly shows a crack in the African Plate—a string of underwater volcanoes and the volcanic belt of the Cameroons.

OUT OF AFRICA

When Pangaea broke up into today's continents, it split along rifts. Africa proves this. The coastlines form a jigsaw fit with those of the other continents from which it split. What's more, Africa is still splitting. The Rift Valley system, which stretches from the Red Sea down to Mozambique, shows where the split is happening.

A rift usually starts as a rise in the Earth's crust from which three cracks radiate out. Two cracks develop the main rift movement, while the third is less active.

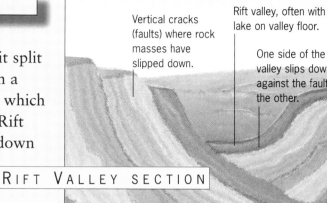

Vertical cracks (faults) where rock masses have slipped down.

Rift valley, often with lake on valley floor.

One side of the rift valley slips down against the fault of the other.

RIFT VALLEY SECTION

Below:
The floor of the Rift Valley in Ethiopia (the Afar Triangle) matches the coastline of Yemen to the northeast.

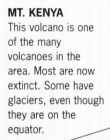

MT. KENYA
This volcano is one of the many volcanoes in the area. Most are now extinct. Some have glaciers, even though they are on the equator.

MADAGASCAR
This large island was once joined to Africa. It is now traveling toward India.

RED SEA RIFT
The opposite shores of the Red Sea match each other. They only overlap in the area of the Afar Triangle, where three cracks diverge.

RIFT LAKES
The great lakes that can be seen from space mark out the Great Rift Valley in East Africa. They are the deepest lakes on the continent.

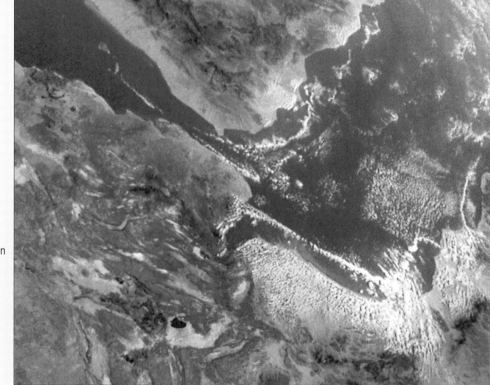

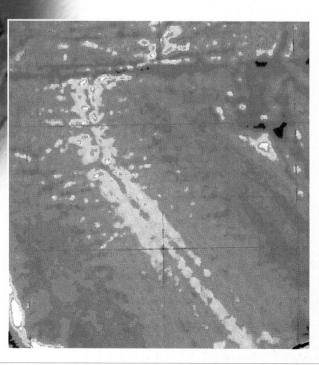

UNDERSEA BACKBONE

New plates are constantly being created along the underwater ocean ridges. Molten rock, known as magma, wells to the surface along a rift and solidifies, forming mountains running parallel to the ridge. This then pulls apart and forms another rift, and more material wells up and solidifies. Over the years, this material builds up into plates that then move away from each other. The youngest part of the plate is closest to the rift, and the oldest is the farthest away.

Left:
The rift along the center of the Mid-Atlantic Ridge. Parallel mountain ridges along each side show where new crust is emplaced.

Building mountains :

See also:
Earth movements p. 16 • **Volcano!** p. 20
Moving plates p. 18 • **Spreading rifts** p. 22

WHEN TWO CONTINENTAL plates collide, it is like a traffic accident—but instead of lasting for a few fractions of a second, the collision takes place over millions of years. The stresses and strains are enormous. The forces have to escape, and in the only direction possible—upward. In this way, mountains are born.

FOUR KINDS OF MOUNTAINS

FOLD MOUNTAINS

BLOCK MOUNTAINS

VOLCANOES

DOME MOUNTAINS

Mountain shapes have been grouped into four basic types. All of them have been formed through the actions of heat and pressure and weathered by wind and water.

Left:
The spiky profile of a young mountain. The most youthful rock lies at the top of the peak. A mere 50 million years ago, these rocks would have been mud and sand at the bottom of the sea. This peak is in the French Alps near the border with Italy.

THE MAKING OF THE HIMALAYAS

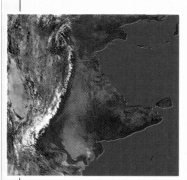

Above:
The Indian sub-continent as viewed by an orbiting satellite.

About 165 million years ago, the Indo-Australian Plate started to move north-ward toward the central Asian Plate. As it hit the older and harder rocks, parts of the younger Indian Plate rose up and over the Asian Plate. At the same time, parts of it were pushed down into the Earth's crust.

The Himalayas are still rising more than .2 inches (5 mm) a year. In a million years, they could be about 3 miles (5 km) higher—even allowing for some weathering.

TIBETAN PLATEAU

Away from the point of impact, the rocks are crumpled up into hills.

"Young" mountains rise up at the point of impact.

Direction of movement.

At the point of impact rocks slip and slide under great pressure. This causes heat to build up and the rock to *metamorphose*, or change, into new rock types. It is at these points that earthquakes may also occur.

Oceanic crust is not as strong as the continental crust with which it collides.

The thinner oceanic crust dives under the older, harder continental rock and melts to form new rocks hundreds of miles (km) below the Earth's surface.

The Himalayan Mountains contain most of the world's peaks higher than 25,000 feet (7,620 m).

Mt. Everest, the world's highest point, rises 29,107 feet (8,872 m) above sea level.

I N D I A N   S U B - C O N T I N E N T

YOUNG AND OLD

"YOUNG" MOUNTAINS
When the shapes of mountains are sharp and jagged, they are called "young." This is Mount Everest.

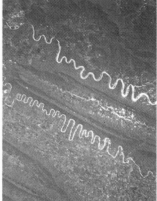

"OLD" MOUNTAINS
The action of natural weathering gradually wears down the sharp edges of the rocks so that they take on a rounded look. At this point, they become known as "old" mountains, like these in central Asia.

This three-dimensional computer model of India shows the Himalayan range in exaggerated perspective to emphasize the massive collision of the two plate boundaries that created the Himalayas. Compare it with the inset picture on the far left.

Shake, rattle, and roll

See also:
- **Earth movements** *p. 16*
- **Moving plates** *p. 18*

Right and far right:
The San Andreas Fault as it appears thousands of feet above the Mojave Desert, which borders the Landers area. At other points it even bisects highways and road systems.

EARTHQUAKES ARE perhaps the most deadly of all the catastrophes that can strike the human race. It is known that over one million quakes shake the earth every year, but most are hardly ever felt.

When two layers of moving rock stick, instead of slide, forces are built up so that eventually the energy is released with explosive force. The point on the surface above where this happens is called the "epicenter."

Energy flows out, like the ripples on a pond after a stone has been thrown into it. These waves, which take different forms, can travel through the rock in seconds. The recent 1989 San Francisco earthquake shook an area of 621,400 square miles, from southern Oregon to Los Angeles.

Earthquake epicenter

Landers township

Main fault lines

Above:
On June 28, 1992, Landers, California, was shaken by an earthquake of 7.3 magnitude. This computer enhancement shows shock waves rippling outward from the quake's epicenter.

THE 'BIG ONE'

For almost a century Californians have been living in dread of the "Big One," an earthquake that will match the 7.7 magnitude shock that toppled San Francisco in 1906. The quake of 1989 in northern California suggested that all would be far from well when the next large tremor strikes. Experts have warned that when the time comes for another tremor it will be preceded by a "seismic silence." Reliable earthquake prediction is still a long way away.

In certain earthquake-prone countries like Italy and Turkey new construction must be of an "earthquake-

THE FAULT LIES IN THE GROUND

There are four main kinds of fault found in rock strata. Each is as deadly as the others. Coupled with the wavelike action of seismic shocks, it is little wonder that the earth shakes and twists.

Strike-slip fault

Normal fault

Thrust fault

SAN FRANCISCO 1906

SAN FRANCISCO 1989

SAN FRANCISCO
Much of the 1989 destruction was caused to buildings sited on land reclaimed after the 1906 earthquake.

SAN ANDREAS FAULT
The fault line can clearly be seen from space as it crosses the San Francisco Bay area. To the left of the picture the fault is particularly visible just above the white-shored cape known as the Point Reyes National Seashore.

proof" standard. Reinforced concrete is now suspect, as under certain conditions it can crumble. In the U.S. engineers are experimenting with frameworks that sway rather than crack, rubber cushions to separate buildings from the ground, and computer-controlled pistons to counteract the earthquake's movement.

Fire almost inevitably follows an earthquake, and emergency services plan accordingly.

The rock story

See also:
- **Volcano!** p. 20
- **Spreading rifts** p. 22
- **Rivers** p. 38
- **...and deltas** p. 42

A S OLD AS THE HILLS—we think of the Earth's crust as indestructible. But in fact, the rocks that make up the mountains and hills are constantly being broken down and rebuilt.

They may have been rebuilt after being melted and resolidified. They may be compressed and "cooked" into completely new types of rock. Or they may be broken down by erosion and fused together into different kinds of rock types. This constant renewing of the Earth's surface is known as the rock cycle.

Above:
The Grand Canyon, carved out by the Colorado River, is 217 miles (350 km) long. Erosion over three million years has laid bare the geological history of the rock in a layer more than 1 mile (1.6 km) deep.

Below:
These basalt rock columns in Northern Ireland are formed from solidified lava that came from a now-extinct volcano. Basalt is an igneous rock.

HOW ROCKS ARE FORMED

Rocks are gradually broken down and eroded by weathering. The debris is slowly washed away and piles up to form a deep layer of sediment.

Through time, this layer of sediment is compressed and compacted by the weight of further layers laid down. Water passing through the sediment lays down minerals between the rock particles, causing chemical and physical changes that cement the particles into a solid mass.

The end result is sedimentary rock, one of the three kinds of rock. Sedimentary rock is formed in horizontal layers, called strata. These become visible when the rock is exposed by river erosion, as in the Grand Canyon, or when hills formed of sedimentary rocks, like the Appalachians, are worn away.

The other two kinds of rock are igneous rock—formed from magma—and metamorphic rock, shaped and compressed by the Earth's forces from preexisting rock.

Metamorphic rock is created when rock buried in the heart of a mountain chain becomes compressed and heated, perhaps through the movement of tectonic plates. The mineral crystals in the rock break down and realign to give new rocks with a different texture. Marble and schist are both metamorphic rocks.

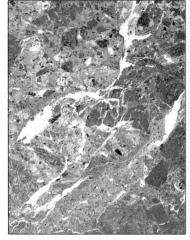

Right:
Marble is an example of metamorphic rock. This rock was once sedimentary limestone, until pressure and heat altered it. The many beautiful colors of marble come from impurities in the original limestone.

BORN IN FIRE

Molten material within the Earth—magma—may squeeze to the surface and erupt through volcanoes or ooze out onto the ocean floor. The magma will cool and solidify into a fine-grained, extrusive igneous rock.

If the magma cools and solidifies before it reaches the surface, it produces an intrusive igneous rock, such as granite. This rock is coarse-grained, with big crystals of minerals in it.

SANDS OF TIME

The different types of sedimentary rock that exist, along with the structures and fossils embedded in them, help us to work out the history of the Earth.

ROCK TYPE
Coarse sediment, such as a shingle beach, becomes the coarse sedimentary rock conglomerate. Sand forms sandstone. Finer silts and mud create siltstone and shale. Chemicals deposited on a seafloor form limestone.

SEDIMENTARY STRUCTURES
Silt drying out in the sun shrivels into cracks, and these can be preserved in the siltstone. Ripples in shore sand and pits formed by rainfall can also be preserved. They are witnesses to ancient climates.

LIFE OF THE PAST
The remains of animals, birds, and plants that lived and died when layers of sediment were laid down are often buried and preserved as fossils. From the evidence of these fossils, we can plot the history of life on Earth.

Right:
A massive amount of silt and sand is transported by rivers. It is then deposited in estuaries and deltas, like the Mekong delta in Vietnam.

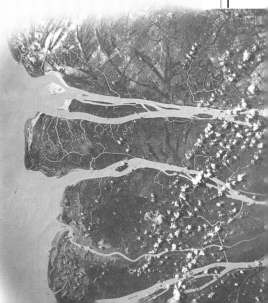

Fallen stars

See also:
- **Earth in space** p. 12
- **Volcano!** p. 20
- **Building mountains** p. 24
- **Shake, rattle, and roll** p. 26

THE EARTH has been bombarded by rocky debris from space—comets and meteorites—ever since the planet was formed. Most meteorites burn up in the atmosphere, but a few are large enough to reach the ground. In recent years, there have been a few "near misses," such as when the comet Shoemaker-Levy tore itself apart going around Jupiter in 1994. What would be the effect on Earth of such a strike? Statistically, it is only a matter of time before another comet threatens our planet.

Above:
Satellite view showing sooty impact site of a possible comet landing on Greenland in December 1997. Comets are made from "dirty snow" and ice, while meteorites are solid rock.

Right:
The massive crater at Manicouagan in Quebec, Canada. The crater is 43 miles (70 km) wide and is thought to be 212 million years old. The meteorite struck the ancient rock of the Canadian Shield, so the crater has not been destroyed by plate movement.

YUCATAN IMPACT SITE

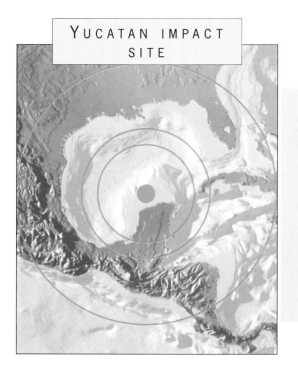

Evidence of iridium deposit marking extent of asteroid impact.

THE BIGGEST HIT YET?

Sixty-five million years ago, something wiped out the dinosaurs and most other life on Earth as well. The culprit was probably a vast meteorite that landed in Chicxulub, Mexico, forming a crater 110 miles (177 km) in diameter. The dust and gases sent high into the atmosphere would have changed the climate for a long time, making the Earth cold and dark. Plants could not have survived, and animals would have starved.

HOW TO MAKE AN IMPRESSION

A meteorite rips into the surface of the Earth with explosive impact, melting a large crater and blasting out debris. The craters on the moon look similar.

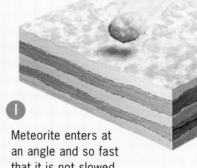

1 Meteorite enters at an angle and so fast that it is not slowed down by the Earth's atmosphere.

2 Rocky "ejecta" is thrown out of the crater made by the colliding meteorite. The heat of the impact fuses and transforms rocks over the whole collision area.

3 A high-profiled edge is thrown up around the crater. Over time, this erodes away.

Dust settles in the impact hole made by the meteorite. A mountain in the center is formed from rock pulled up by the explosion.

Below:
Meteor Crater in Arizona was made about 10,000 years ago. It is more than 590 feet (180 m) deep and about three-quarters of a mile (1.2 km) in diameter. An impact like this on a city is unimaginable.

Squashed forests

See also:
- ...**lakes** p. 40
- ...**and deltas** p. 42
- **Changing coasts** p. 62

Below:
The swamp forests of the coal ages were similar to the modern delta swamps of the equatorial rain forest.

COAL IS FOSSILIZED PLANT material. For millions of years, swamp forests on Earth absorbed the energy of the sun and the carbon dioxide of the atmosphere as they grew. When the trees died, they were buried by other plant material and, due to the lack of oxygen, did not rot away. After millions of years of compression, the carbon in this material turned into coal. Nowadays, when we burn coal, we release the energy that was stored all those millions of years ago.

Left:
A fossil leaf, typical of the plants that formed the Carboniferous period forest.

As vegetation dies off, it sinks into the muddy swamp water. Layers of this organic debris build up over the centuries.

HOW A SWAMP BECOMES COAL

A layer of dead plant material is buried in river sand. Over millions of years, this layer is compressed as other layers are formed on top of it. As the sand turns to sandstone, the plant material loses much of its hydrogen and oxygen, and the carbon becomes more condensed. The greater the proportion of carbon, the higher the grade of coal.

Peat is formed as the dead vegetation loses its moisture and becomes more compressed.

COAL IN NORTH AMERICA

Most of the world's coal was formed in the Carboniferous period, about 300 million years ago.

At this time, newly formed mountain ranges were eroding, spreading sediment across the shallow seas. This produced large areas of delta, which in turn were covered with swamp forests.

Coal from this period is found in eastern North America, in Pennsylvania and Ohio. Coal from the later Permian period is found in the Great Plains and further west, on into the Rockies.

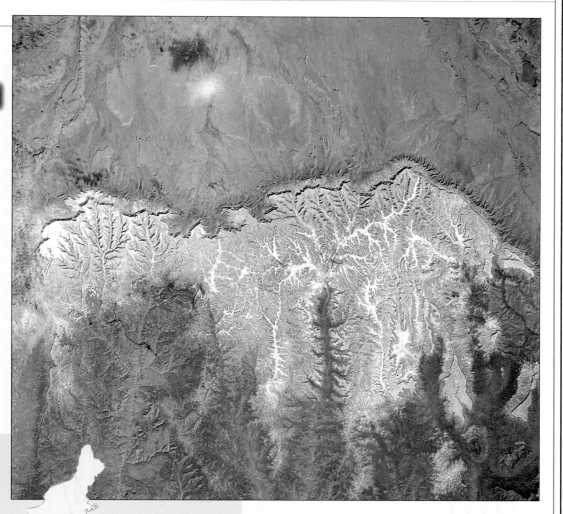

COAL ZONES IN THE USA

Key

Carboniferous outcrops ■

Permian outcrops □

Above:
Many coalfields, such as Black Mesa in the Arizona Desert, come from the Permian period, which is more recent. Permian coal is of a lower grade.

When these fields are close to the surface, they can be mined by the opencast method.

Deep shaft coal mine

Opencast coal mine

Over millions of years, peat becomes coal through a process of compression and chemical change.

Black gold

See also:
- **Squashed forests** p. 32
- ...lakes p. 40
- **...and deltas** p. 42
- **Changing coasts** p. 62

Above:
Oil and gas move through porous rocks, usually floating upward through the reservoir rock. They are lost at the surface unless they are caught in rock structures called traps. The Zagros Mountains of Iran (above) and other areas of the Middle East are full of these traps, giving rise to the great oil industry of the area.

Left:
Oil refinery tanks and pipelines in Saudi Arabia.

Much of today's economy in the West is based on oil. Oil is used as a fuel and a power source, and it is also a valuable raw material: a vast range of plastics are made from oil.

Like coal, oil is a fossil fuel, formed from the remains of tiny sea creatures that were buried on the seafloor under layers of sediment where lack of oxygen prevented the normal process of decay. Bacterial action and heat from within the Earth broke down these substances into a series of carbon compounds, trapped within the underground rock.

These carbon compounds are the raw materials that make up gas and oil. Once the gas and oil have formed into large pockets underground, they can then be extracted.

THE CLUE OF THE SALT DOMES

Oil traps are usually found where the rocks are buckled upward in curved structures. The oil can gather beneath, like air in an upturned cup in a sinkful of water. The crumpled, oil-bearing rocks of the Arabian Gulf have many traps, including those formed by "salt domes."

Since layers of salt are lighter than other rocks, they tend to rise through other rock layers, twisting them up as they go. The twisted beds form ideal traps, and it is structures like this that oil geologists look for.

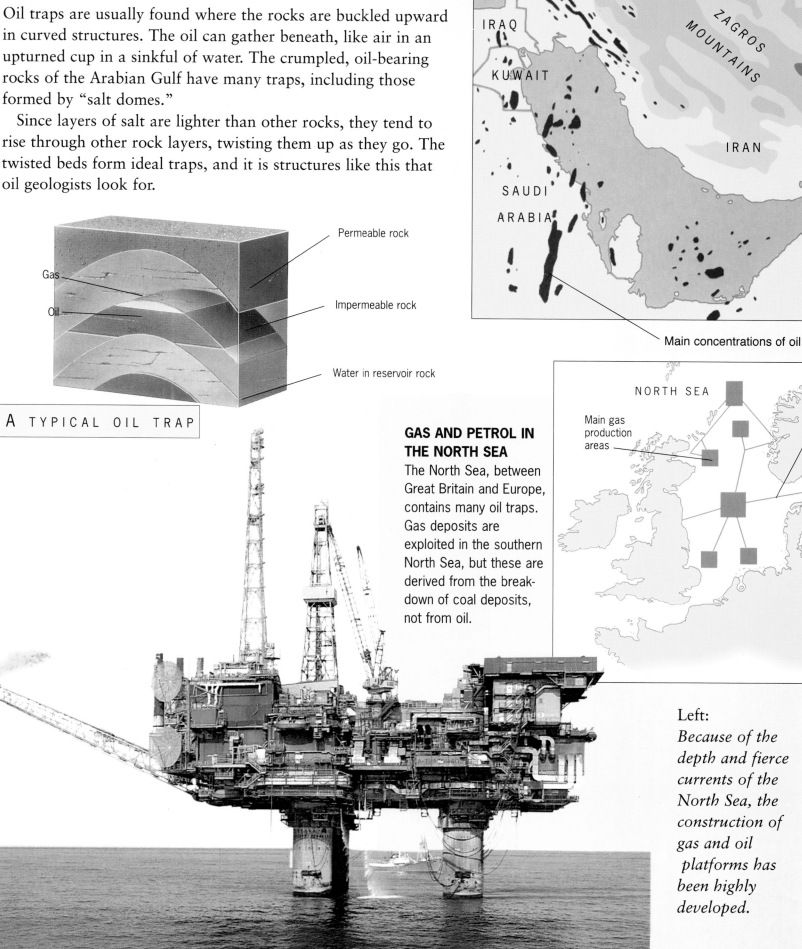

Permeable rock

Gas

Oil

Impermeable rock

Water in reservoir rock

A TYPICAL OIL TRAP

Main concentrations of oil

IRAQ

KUWAIT

SAUDI ARABIA

ZAGROS MOUNTAINS

IRAN

GAS AND PETROL IN THE NORTH SEA
The North Sea, between Great Britain and Europe, contains many oil traps. Gas deposits are exploited in the southern North Sea, but these are derived from the break-down of coal deposits, not from oil.

NORTH SEA

Main gas production areas

Main gas pipelines

Left:
Because of the depth and fierce currents of the North Sea, the construction of gas and oil platforms has been highly developed.

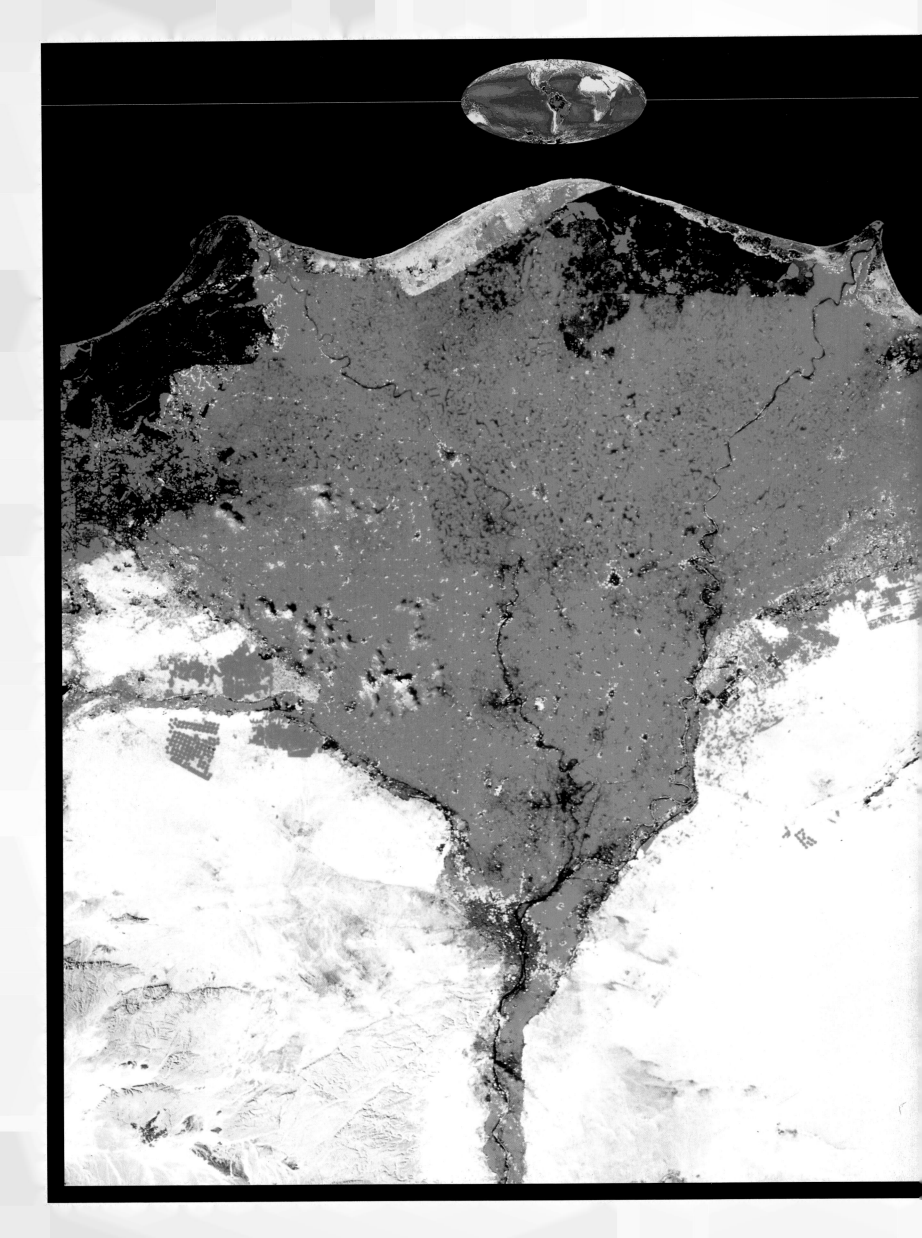

PART TWO

Earth in action

The Earth changes before our eyes: Water carves out channels through and under the ground, desert sands shift in the wind. . . .

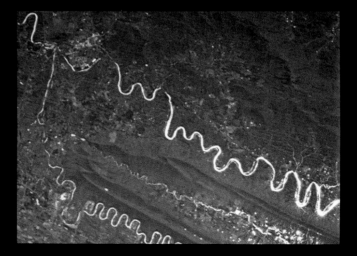

Rivers

See also:
- ...lakes p. 40
- ...and deltas p. 42
- Eroding earth p. 44
- Changing coasts p. 62

Below:
Rivers can modify the landscape through the processes of erosion and deposition. Typically, a river goes through three stages—the first is erosion, the third is deposition, and the second is a balance between the two, as shown by the photographs.

RIVERS ARE AN ESSENTIAL part of the water cycle on Earth. The sun evaporates water from the surfaces of the oceans. This water vapor is then blown over the continents by the winds.

When the atmosphere changes in pressure or in temperature, the water vapor condenses into clouds and falls as rain or snow. The water falling on the land eventually runs together to produce rivers that carry it back to the oceans once more. These cycles continue every second of every day and have done so for millions of years.

FIRST STAGE

SECOND STAGE

RIVER VALLEY
After passing through its first stage, the energy of the river is reduced. It can still erode a valley, but most erosion takes place at the sides, and the valley tends to be broad. This is the Shenandoah River in Virginia.

MOUNTAIN STREAM
A quickly flowing stream in the Alps is full of energy as it rushes down the mountainside, eroding its bed into a deep ravine. The eroded rock is picked up and carried along, adding to the erosive force.

FLOOD PLAIN
Eroded material begins to fall to the riverbed as the current slackens, and soil and mud are laid on the valley floor. When it floods, whole sheets of sediment are deposited, creating a flat-bottomed valley over which the river meanders.

RIVER STAGES AND SHAPES

In the river's first stage, where it runs in a deep, V-shaped gorge, there is no depositing of material, only erosion.

In the second stage, where the river runs across layers of its own sediment, it is deeper on the outside curves, where the current is faster. It gradually erodes the outside of the curves and deposits sediment on the inside, so constantly changing its course.

In the third stage, so much sediment is deposited that the river may be above the level of the plain, held back by levees (banks of sediment deposited during floods).

FIRST STAGE CROSS SECTION

SECOND STAGE CROSS SECTION

THIRD STAGE CROSS SECTION

THIRD STAGE

SPENT POWER
In the last stage of its life, the river has lost most of its power. It slowly meanders across the land in great loops, often cut off as oxbow lakes. Mud and silt are deposited on the flood-plain or near the river's mouth, as here on the coastal plain of Sarawak.

...lakes

See also:
- **Volcano!** *p. 20*
- **Spreading rifts** *p. 22*
- **Rivers** *p. 38*
- **...and deltas** *p. 42*

Below:
Lakes form in the hollows gouged out by the weight of passing glaciers. Glaciers can also deposit rocky material (moraine), forming dams that hold back the water from the melting ice. The Great Lakes of North America are examples of huge glacier lakes.

THERE ARE THREE main kinds of lake: lakes scooped out by glaciers; lakes formed in hollows produced by the movements of the Earth, such as the Rift Valley lakes; and lakes formed where rivers flow into an inland basin. There are also artificial lakes, formed when a river is dammed, or when lagoons are cut off from the sea. Most lakes are freshwater, but some may accumulate minerals and become saltier than the sea. There are probably more lakes on the Earth's surface now than at any time in its history.

THE PRESENT DAY

Lake Erie was once the most polluted body of water in the world, because of industrial effluent flowing into it. Now, with strict environmental controls, the water is clear once more.

Today, the Chicago River flows into Lake Michigan, rather than out of it as it did 11,000 years ago. If the continent of North America continues to tilt, it may flow out again in 1,500 years' time.

Below:
Over time, the margins of lakes become overgrown with vegetation. This gradually encroaches on the water until the lake becomes a swamp, or even covered over entirely.

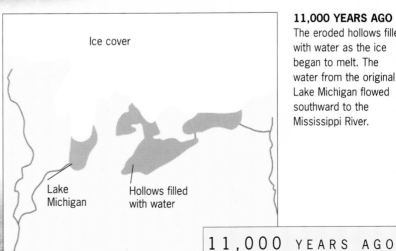

Ice cover

Lake Michigan

Hollows filled with water

11,000 YEARS AGO
The eroded hollows filled with water as the ice began to melt. The water from the original Lake Michigan flowed southward to the Mississippi River.

11,000 YEARS AGO

LAKES FROM EARTH MOVEMENTS

Lake Baikal in Siberia is a typical rift valley lake. The rift valley was formed by plate movements that are slowly tearing Asia apart. As the valley has formed over the last 50 million years, it has filled with water, making it the oldest lake on Earth.

Other earth-movement lakes include the crater lakes of extinct volcanoes, where the empty cone fills up with water. Crater Lake in Oregon is a good example, as are the maars of the Eifel district in Germany.

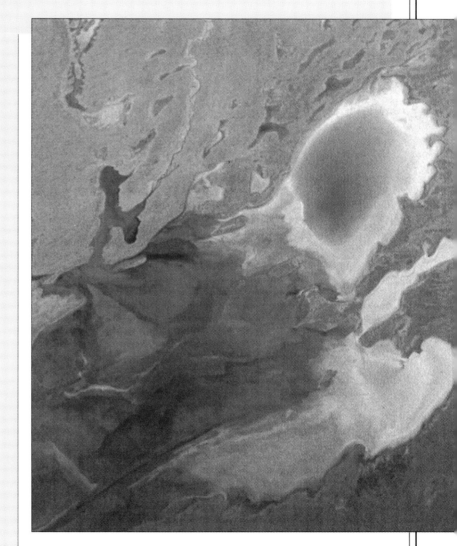

HOW THE LAKES BECAME GREAT

At the height of the last Ice Age, half of North America was covered with ice. The ice sheet advanced southward, scouring the surface and carrying along rubble and debris embedded in the ice. When the ice melted at the end of the Ice Age, the hollows left behind were filled with water and became the Great Lakes. At certain times in the past the Great Lakes were much more extensive than they are at present—shown by the presence of raised beaches. These lakes are estimated to contain about 20 percent of the world's freshwater.

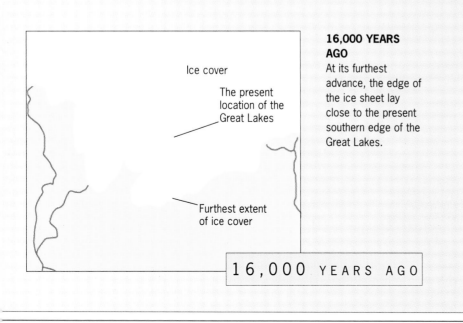

Ice cover

The present location of the Great Lakes

Furthest extent of ice cover

16,000 YEARS AGO
At its furthest advance, the edge of the ice sheet lay close to the present southern edge of the Great Lakes.

16,000 YEARS AGO

AUSTRALIA'S GREAT SALT LAKE

In desert areas, the rivers from surrounding hills may flow into inland basins and form a lake in the wet season.

In the dry season, all the water evaporates away, leaving plains of salt. This example is Lake Eyre in southern Australia. Others exist in Death Valley, California.

...and deltas

See also:
- **Rivers** *p. 38*
- **...lakes** *p. 40*
- **Eroding earth** *p. 44*
- **Changing coasts** *p. 62*

Below:

The great sprawling mass of green in the desert shows the Okavango delta at the edge of the Kalahari Desert basin. Most deltas are formed at the mouth of a river where it flows into the sea. This is a rare example of an inland delta, built up during the rainy seasons.

THE INLAND DELTA

In Botswana, southern Africa, the Okavango River forms an inland delta as it spreads out at the edge of the vast, semi-arid Kalahari Desert. Its seasonal watery fingers stretch out over 805 square miles (2,085 sq km).

In the rainy season, water flows down to this delta and plant life flourishes. Grazing animals migrate there to feed as a relief from the dry conditions in the surrounding desert plains.

AS A RIVER FLOWS into the sea, it brings with it much of the sand and silt that it has picked up on its journey. If there are no strong tides or currents to wash it away, this sediment sinks to the bottom, building up gradually into sandbanks.

The river then gradually changes its course to find a way through, and may split up into many shifting channels. The result is a delta. The name was first given by the Ancient Greeks to the mouth of the Nile, which is shaped like the Greek letter Δ.

Deltas are very fertile, because of the rich silt, and have always attracted human settlement. Cairo, New Orleans, and Calcutta are all built on deltas.

THE MAKING OF THE NILE DELTA

Five and a half million years ago, the Mediterranean Sea did not exist. The Nile River flowed from Africa onto a low desert plain which lay between North Africa and Europe. Over time, the river laid down a huge alluvial "fan" of sediment. Today, most of the eastern Mediterranean seafloor is made of this sediment.

The fertile silt, along with the constant water supply, means that the Nile delta has been cultivated throughout history. However, its character is changing. The number of irrigation ditches in the delta has increased, and the flow of the Nile is now controlled by the Aswan Dam, starving the delta of new sediment. As a result, the front of the delta is now being eroded away.

5.5 MILLION YEARS AGO

800,000 YEARS AGO

THE PRESENT DAY

Above:
The Nile delta can clearly be seen from space. In recent years, the delta has become clogged with plants, giving the Egyptians problems in how best to manage the changing environment.

RIVER AND MAN

The Mississippi delta is what is known as a "bird's foot" delta. Its pattern is formed by the river channels forming levees (high banks of sediment) which reach out into the waters of the Gulf of Mexico.

Because the floor of the Gulf of Mexico is subsiding, much of the sediment carried out to sea is spreading out on the seafloor, and the levees are left to form the delta.

Today, the Mississippi River exits eastward, via New Orleans. But if there had been no human intervention to maintain the existing channels, it would have swung south again by now.

Eroding earth

See also:
- **Volcano!** p. 20
- **Spreading rifts** p. 22
- **Rivers** p. 38
- **...and deltas** p. 42

Below:
The Dalmatian coastline in Slovenia consists of islands and inlets running parallel to the shore, formed by the eroded ridges and valleys of parallel mountain ranges. The limestone rocks have gradually been eroded and dissolved by water.

As soon as rocks are lifted above sea level, the forces of nature combine to wear them away in a process known as erosion.

Physical erosion takes place when the sheer forces of the elements—wind, rain, ice, or sea waves—act on the rock to break it up and carry off the fragments.

In chemical erosion, there is a chemical reaction between the minerals contained in the rocks and the atmosphere, causing the rocks to crumble and collapse.

FORCES AT WORK

A TYPICAL CAVE SYSTEM

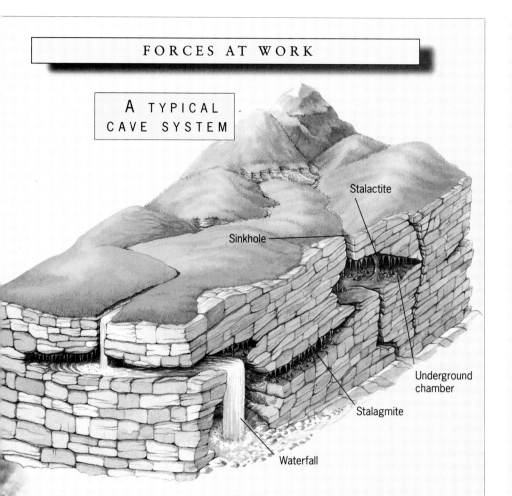

Stalactite

Sinkhole

Underground chamber

Stalagmite

Waterfall

Limestone is a porous rock that is very vulnerable to chemical weathering. Its main component is calcium carbonate, which is broken down by the acid in rainwater into calcium hydrocarbonate, which then dissolves in the water.

The end result is a "karst" landscape, named after a region in Slovenia, where the barren limestone is dissolved into hollows and cracks, and the rocks beneath are riddled with potholes, caves, and caverns carved out by the water.

SPECTACULAR EFFECTS

A limestone cavern is shaped as the limestone is dissolved by the acid in rainwater. Horizontal galleries form along the water table and can be left dry if the water table drops. Side caves are eroded along joints and bedding planes in the rock where it is most vulnerable.

Right:
Water passing through limestone can build as well as destroy. The dissolved calcite in groundwater can be deposited on the walls and roofs of caves, forming spectacular stalagmites growing up, and stalactites coming down.

LANDSLIDES AND WATER

The most dramatic form of physical erosion is through landslides. These occur when a slope becomes unstable. Landslides can be triggered in several ways.

Very often, human activities cause landslides. A landslide in Naples in 1998 happened because there was no control on building, and too many houses were built on a slope that was not strong enough to support them.

In some areas, the soil on a slope becomes unstable when vegetation is removed—particularly when trees are felled. Rainwater gradually loosens the soil until, eventually, a mass of mud slides downhill, often with disastrous results.

SOIL CREEP This is slow erosion through the gradual movement of soil and other particles downhill.

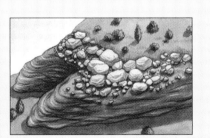

MUD SLIDES These occur on a slope when trees are felled, and loose soil is then mixed with water during a storm.

SCREE This is a rubbly slope of broken rocks, split away from a hillside through the action of frost.

CLIFF SLUMPS A mass of solid rock cracks and slides downward along a curved surface.

Shifting deserts

See also:
- **Polar regions** *p. 48*
- **Frozen earth** *p. 52*
- **Moving bands** *p. 54*
- **El Niño** *p. 58*

KUISEB RIVER BOUNDARY
The Kuiseb River washes the creeping sand into the ocean. Coastal sand spits show the northward-flowing cold current that produces the typical coastal desert conditions.

THE GREAT SAND SEA
The pattern of dunes in the Namib Desert shows how the prevailing winds are constantly moving the sand northward.

Above:
The sheer size and intense color of the great Namib Desert makes it easy to identify from the space shuttle.

The three different kinds of desert are all to be found within its boundaries.

Deserts occur where there is very little rainfall— usually less than 10 inches (25 cm) per year, falling in one brief season. Most deserts are hot, but some, such as the Taklamakan Desert in China, can be found in cold areas. They can also be found on the tops of high plateaus that get little rainfall.

The popular image of a desert as a place where nothing grows is actually quite rare. Desert vegetation can consist of very poor grassland or scrub, and succulent plants such as cacti.

SKELETON COAST

The Namib is a coastal desert, formed by the cold sea currents flowing from the Antarctic. The cold sea cools the air above and causes it to descend. As rain only falls from ascending air, this produces dry desert conditions.

Toward the east, the Namib Desert merges into the Kalahari, a tropical desert. Warm air rises at the equator, dropping all its moisture as rain and producing rain forest. As this dry air drifts away from the equator, it cools and descends at the latitude of the Tropics, producing the tropical desert belts.

DESERT ZONES

Tropical deserts form along the Tropics, where dry air descends. These include the Sahara and Mexican deserts along the Tropic of Cancer, and the Kalahari and Australian deserts along the Tropic of Capricorn.

Continental deserts, such as the Gobi, are dry because of their distance from the sea. Coastal deserts such as the Atacama and the Namib form where cold ocean currents flow toward the equator.

Rain shadow deserts, such as those in California and Patagonia, lie in the lee of mountains where only dry air reaches them.

Key

Tropical

Continental

Rain shadow

Cold

ROCKY AND STONY DESERTS

The Namib Desert is an example of the three kinds of desert. It not only has sand but also contains stretches of stony desert pavement and exposed bedrock with little soil.

THREE KINDS OF DESERT

Within the various desert zones there are three different types of desert, each producing its own distinctive landforms.

Wind is the most powerful agent in the formation of desert landscapes.

SAND DESERT
The sand sea is the most familiar desert type. Wind erosion reduces exposed rocks to sand, blown along in slow waves called dunes.

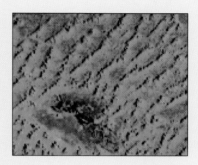

STONY DESERT
The stony desert, or pavement, is a surface of wind-polished stones. This may be only a surface crust, sealing off a layer of finer dust.

ROCKY DESERT
Dry desert conditions mean that few plants grow, and no soil can form. The bedrock of the landscape is exposed and eroded.

60°N

Turkmenistan

Gobi

Iran

Mojave

Taklamakan

30°N

Chihuahua

Thar

Sahara

Arabia

Somalia

Equator

Atacama

Australian deserts

Namib

Kalahari

30°S

Monte

Patagonia

60°S

Antarctica

THE DESERT AREAS OF THE WORLD

Polar regions

See also:
- **Volcano!** *p. 20*
- **Spreading rifts** *p. 22*
- **Rivers of ice** *p. 50*
- **Holes in the sky** *p. 76*

Below and right:
The two great masses of Antarctica (right) and the Arctic (below) are shown here on satellite images. The Arctic is mainly frozen sea. Antarctica is a landmass covered by an ice sheet.

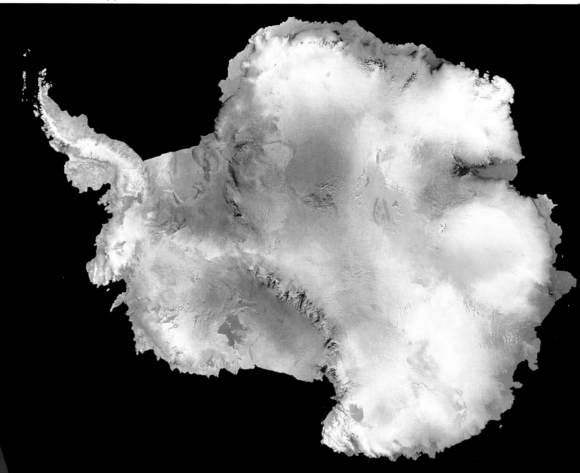

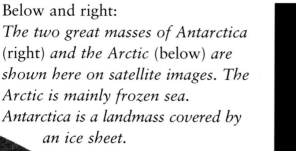

THE TWO GREAT MASSES of ice at either end of the planet hold well over 90 percent of the world's ice. Each year, as the globe gets warmer, the ice shrinks and the oceans get deeper. In Antarctica, the average thickness of the ice is 6,500 feet (2,000 m). In the Arctic, the sea ice is 10–16 feet (3–5 m) thick.

There are no volcanoes in the Arctic, but five active ones have been found in Antarctica.

Below:
Arctic icebergs float away into the North Atlantic Ocean. These icebergs are sharply shaped, unlike their flat-topped Antarctic cousins.

FIVE VARIETIES OF ICE

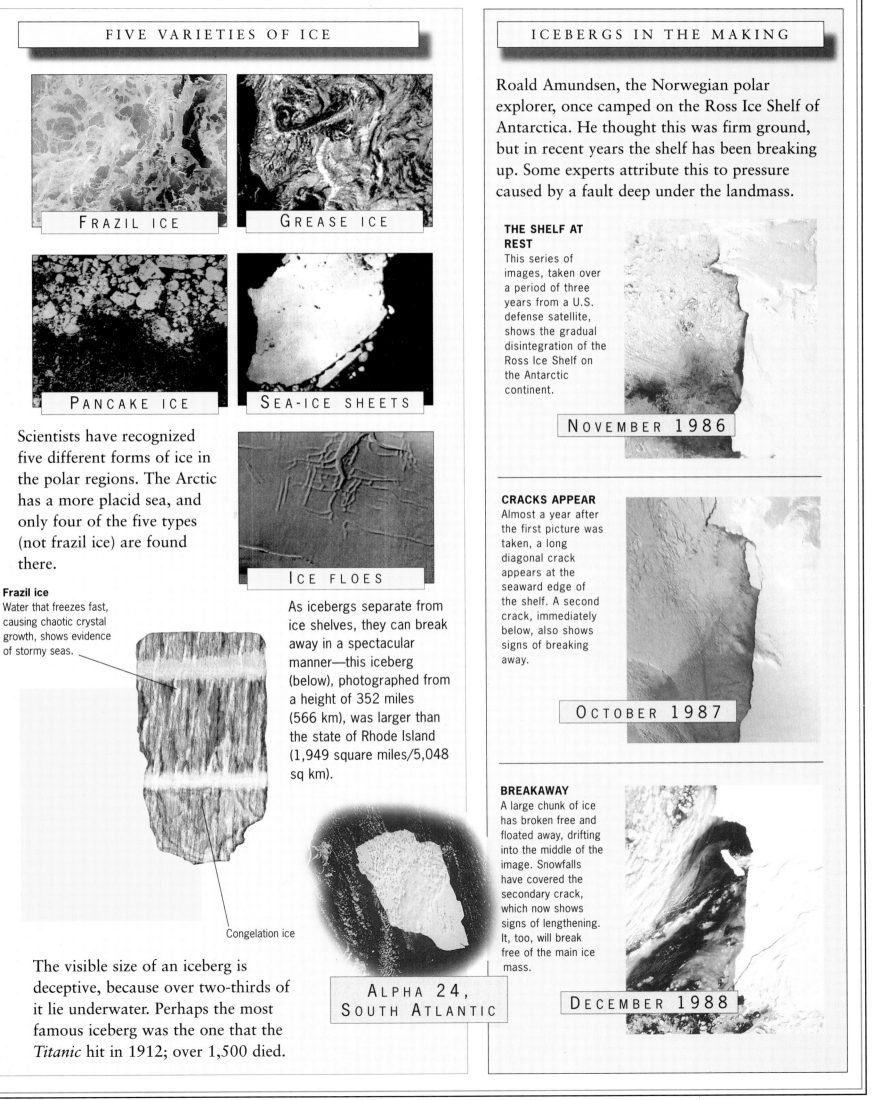

FRAZIL ICE

GREASE ICE

PANCAKE ICE

SEA-ICE SHEETS

ICE FLOES

Scientists have recognized five different forms of ice in the polar regions. The Arctic has a more placid sea, and only four of the five types (not frazil ice) are found there.

Frazil ice
Water that freezes fast, causing chaotic crystal growth, shows evidence of stormy seas.

Congelation ice

As icebergs separate from ice shelves, they can break away in a spectacular manner—this iceberg (below), photographed from a height of 352 miles (566 km), was larger than the state of Rhode Island (1,949 square miles/5,048 sq km).

The visible size of an iceberg is deceptive, because over two-thirds of it lie underwater. Perhaps the most famous iceberg was the one that the *Titanic* hit in 1912; over 1,500 died.

ALPHA 24, SOUTH ATLANTIC

ICEBERGS IN THE MAKING

Roald Amundsen, the Norwegian polar explorer, once camped on the Ross Ice Shelf of Antarctica. He thought this was firm ground, but in recent years the shelf has been breaking up. Some experts attribute this to pressure caused by a fault deep under the landmass.

THE SHELF AT REST
This series of images, taken over a period of three years from a U.S. defense satellite, shows the gradual disintegration of the Ross Ice Shelf on the Antarctic continent.

NOVEMBER 1986

CRACKS APPEAR
Almost a year after the first picture was taken, a long diagonal crack appears at the seaward edge of the shelf. A second crack, immediately below, also shows signs of breaking away.

OCTOBER 1987

BREAKAWAY
A large chunk of ice has broken free and floated away, drifting into the middle of the image. Snowfalls have covered the secondary crack, which now shows signs of lengthening. It, too, will break free of the main ice mass.

DECEMBER 1988

Rivers of ice

See also:
- **Building mountains** p. 24
- **...lakes** p. 40
- **Polar regions** p. 48
- **Changing coasts** p. 62

Below:

This image from a Landsat satellite shows part of the Byrd Glacier in Antarctica. The ice floe can be seen oozing out between the mountain ranges, together with the dark streaks of moraine (rocky debris).

GLACIERS ARE the "plows of the Earth." The raw power they harness rips up the land beneath and crumbles it into powdered rock. Glaciers shape the earth over which they move by carving out huge valleys over millions of years. They can transport rock boulders weighing hundreds of tons and then deposit them, as the glacier slowly melts, many miles away. Although glaciers are so powerful, most move less than 3 feet (1 m) in a year.

These rivers of ice can be many miles wide and stretch for immense distances. They cover almost 11 percent of the Earth's land surface.

WHERE TO FIND ICE

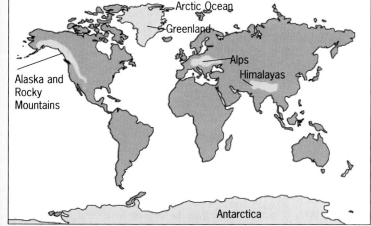

Arctic Ocean

Greenland

Alps

Himalayas

Alaska and Rocky Mountains

Antarctica

Over 6 million square miles (15.5 million sq km) of Earth are permanently covered with ice, including Arctic sea ice, Antarctic and Greenland ice sheets, ice caps, ice shelves, and high-altitude glaciers.

THE ANATOMY OF A GLACIER

Snow gathers in a hollow, or cirque, at the top of a mountain. As the snow builds up, it spills over and slowly flows down like a river. Crevasses, or cracks, form where the angle of the slope changes. Rocky debris—moraine—is left at the sides and at the foot.

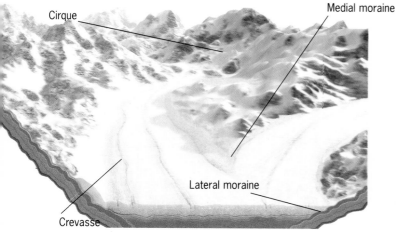

Cirque

Medial moraine

Lateral moraine

Crevasse

Above:
A sinister puff of snow that can signal death and destruction in a few fleeting moments.

Left:
The Cook Glacier in New Zealand's South Island shows many of its classic glacial landscape features from space.

AVALANCHE!

In a moment, a puff of snow and a distant rumble can herald the onset of an avalanche.

One of the worst avalanches of recent years occurred in Peru in 1962, when three million tons of debris from the glacial ice mass above Mt. Huascaran fell onto the slope of the main glacier and cascaded down onto the villages in the valley below. This avalanche of rock, ice, and mud, already about 45 feet (14 m) high, gathered more debris as it descended down the valley. When its journey ended two minutes later, 2,400 people were dead.

Frozen earth

See also:
- **Polar regions** *p. 48*
- **Rivers of ice** *p. 50*
- **Moving bands** *p. 54*
- **The North & South Poles** *p. 88*

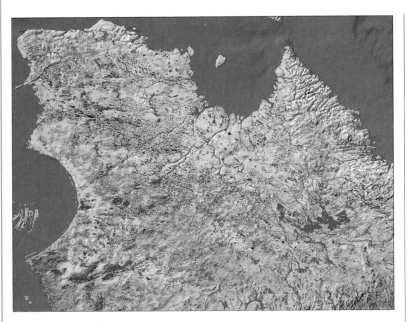

IN THE NORTHERN hemisphere, the last vegetation zone after the tree line and before the ice cap is known as tundra. In the southern hemisphere, only the southern tip of South America has tundra—Antarctica is almost totally covered in ice.

These northern plains are covered with snow and ice in the winter. In the short summer, the ice and snow melt, but the water cannot drain away, and so great areas of lake, pond, and marsh develop in the tundra areas of Alaska, Canada, and Siberia.

Above and right:
Two views of the Canadian tundra taken from a Landsat orbiter in false color (above) and from the space shuttle (right). The bleakness of this land is well conveyed in these color images.

Below:
The great landmass of Asia in summer, showing the tundra regions. Reindeer and musk ox find enough to eat in the mosses, grasses, and lichens in the summer, but migrate south to the forests in the winter.

Above:
Repeated freezing and thawing breaks the topsoil into polygons, as shown here at Spitzbergen.

BOUNDARIES IN ICE

There are no tall trees in the tundra and, because the ground is frozen for most of the year, it has a very short growing season. Mosses, lichens, and grasses are the only vegetation that appears in the summer. The few trees that survive are stunted, because they cannot grow in the long, dark winter with its icy winds. As the tundra nears the polar region, the trees disappear altogether.

Limit of tree line around the northern polar region

ICE POWER

There is a permanently frozen layer of soil, called permafrost, at tundra latitudes. In Siberia and Canada, the permafrost can be 1,650 feet (500 m) deep. Because it remains frozen even in summer, when the surface soil thaws out, the meltwater cannot drain away. Repeated freezing and thawing of the top layer of soil creates patterns of stones on the surface—polygons—and low hills, known as pingoes. Pingoes are mounds of ice that are constantly enlarging from below, stressing and cracking the crust of soil on the top.

PERMAFROST SLICE

Soil thaws in the summer

Permafrost (permanently frozen soil)

Right:
Tombstone Valley in the Yukon, Alaska, is set alight by autumn color. For a few short weeks the low scrub, plants, and lichen transform the tundra wilderness into a blaze of Technicolor tints.

Moving bands

See also:
- **...lakes** *p. 40*
- **and deltas** *p. 42*

- **Shifting deserts** *p. 46*

Above:
A composite image of the Earth, showing how vegetation and habitats form a mirror image north and south of the equator.

THE NATURAL VEGETATION ZONES of the Earth closely follow the climate zones, because plant life is very much controlled by climate. Hot and wet conditions, as along the equator, produce forest. In seasonal dry conditions, grasses and grassy plains thrive, but not trees. In dry climates, only desert vegetation is found. Very cold climates produce forests of conifers—trees that can withstand freezing conditions and shake off heavy coverings of snow.

WHY THERE ARE SEASONS

The Earth's axis is tilted at an angle to its orbit around the sun, so at one time of year the North Pole is pointing toward the sun, and six months later it is pointing away. While the North Pole is pointing toward the sun the northern hemisphere absorbs more sunlight—it is summer in the north and winter in the south. Six months later the situation is reversed.

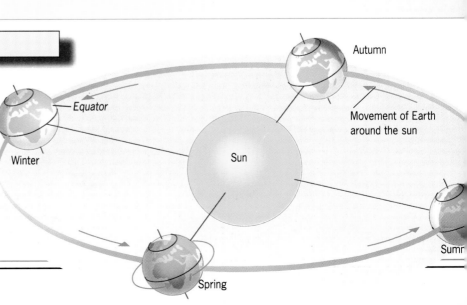

Autumn

Equator

Movement of Earth
around the sun

Winter

Sun

Summ

Spring

New York   London   Omsk   Singapore

Rainfall

Temperature

The colors in the diagram represent the many kinds of climates in the world. Although they look complex and inter-linked, the same broad bands of vegetation reflect each other north and south of the equator.

SUN AND RAIN

The main factors that affect climate, and therefore vegetation, are temperature and humidity.

The climate in the various parts of the world is determined by how much sunlight each area receives, and how much rain falls at different times of the year.

The distance from the equator is a factor in this, as is the position in relation to the prevailing winds that may or may not bring moisture from the oceans.

Rainfall

Temperature

CLIMATE ZONES

Right:
The charts in this diagram show typical rainfall and temperatures throughout the world.

Manaus   Alice Springs   Lagos

TEMPERATE TAKEOVER

No open land will remain barren for long if it is possible for plants to grow. At the end of the last Ice Age, about 10,000 years ago, the land left by the retreating glaciers was quickly colonized by vegetation.

First to come were small plants such as mosses and lichens, which started to create a soil. Then came tough grasses and heathers. The first trees were small, hardy types such as birch and rowan, followed by conifers. Then, as the climate improved, deciduous forest was established.

Open land   Small plants and grass   Scrubland and coarse grasses   Coniferous woodland   Deciduous woodland

Ocean currents

See also:
- **Rivers** *p. 38*
- **and deltas** *p. 42*
- **Seas and tides** *p. 60*
- **Changing coasts** *p. 62*

MORE THAN TWO-THIRDS of the surface of the Earth is covered with water, and this water is in constant motion. Surface currents are driven by the winds, while the deep currents are driven by the circulation of warm and cold water, and by the Coriolis effect. These powerful currents move water across entire oceans, bringing warm weather to cold coastal areas and cooling regions that would otherwise be hot.

MEDDIES
Every time the tide goes in and out of the Mediterranean, it surges between the Straits of Gibraltar, creating pulses of water with a different salinity from those that exist in the Atlantic Ocean. These pulses are known as "Meddies."

ICEBERG CARRIERS
The coast off Labrador has a cold, southerly ocean current that brings with it drifting icebergs, calved from Greenland and the neighboring Labrador coast. More than 700 icebergs move south on this current each year, some traveling many hundreds of miles.

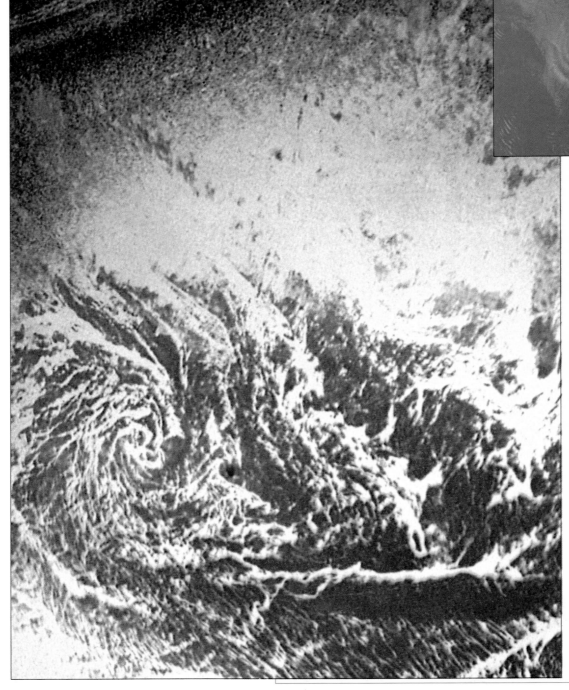

This page:
The ocean can provide many surprising images, as these pictures show. The different currents and depths of the water can show as distinct patterns, even on handheld space shuttle images, helping oceanographers to plot the movements of these vast bodies of water.

PACIFIC SWIRL
This mass of swirling water, glinting in the sun in the Sea of Japan, is many hundreds of miles wide and forms part of a gyre. It is formed by the meeting of the Kuroshia, Oyashio, and North Pacific Currents.

OCEAN CORKSCREWS

The surface currents of the oceans are controlled by the global wind pattern. The main ocean current is called a gyre. These currents sweep around the ocean basins, moving clockwise in the northern hemisphere and counterclockwise in the southern hemisphere.

The various "legs" of a gyre produce warm currents along the western sides of the oceans and cold currents along the eastern sides.

In the North Atlantic, the western current is the Gulf Stream. It brings warm water across the Atlantic from the West Indies to northern Europe.

Hot currents   Cold currents

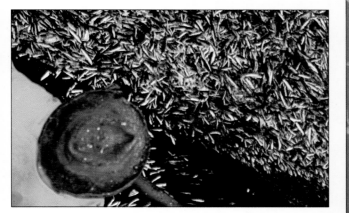

Above:
The cold, deep ocean currents, such as those in the North Atlantic and the Eastern Pacific, are rich in nutrients and so support vast shoals of fish.

SHIFTING SANDS

Ocean currents have a strong influence on the shape of the coastline. When currents move in one prevailing direction, they constantly move the sand along the shoreline in that direction.

In this way, sandbars are gradually built out from the land in gentle sweeps and curves. When the current sweeps past a bay, the sandbar curves back in a sort of hook as eddies swirl around the tip. The bar is a constantly shifting piece of land. England's Spurn Point has rebuilt itself six or seven times over the course of the last 200 years.

Below:
Cape Cod in Massachusetts is a sand spit with a characteristic curve at the tip. It is one of many spits produced by the North Atlantic Drift.

El Niño

See also:
- **Ocean currents** *p. 56*
- **Global weather** *p. 68*
- **Clouds and storms** *p. 70*

MARCH 17, 1997

FIRST WAVE
The progress of the 1997–98 El Niño was charted by false-color photographs taken by the U.S. National Oceanographic and Atmospheric Administration satellite.

MARCH 21, 1997

BUILDUP
The first photograph above (March 17) shows the warm water (shown in red and white) in the equatorial west Pacific. Four days later (right), the warm water was beginning to reach eastward.

THE NORTHEAST AND SOUTHEAST trade winds in the Pacific combine to drive the warm surface water westward. Every few years, however, these waters change direction and flow eastward instead. This change in the ocean circulation, because of a lessenir in the wind strength, has side effects on the climate all over the globe. The effect is known a *El Niño*, or the child, because it often happens around Christmas.

MAKING WAVES

In the past, an El Niño event occurred once in ten years or so. The trade winds lessened in strength, and the warm surface waters accumulated in the west began to move eastward, pooling in the east Pacific and beginning El Niño. This unaccustomed warm water in the eastern Pacific prevented the usual rise of cold water from the deep trenches of the ocean bed. Since the 1990s, El Niño has became so frequent and long lasting, it has almost become the norm. It is likely to have enduring effects on the world's climate.

Above:
Even as far away as Africa, El Niño has upset the continent's balance of sun and rain.

EVENT HORIZON
A month later, the warm water had reached the coast of South America, bringing unseasonal warm conditions to the Galápagos Islands and to Peru, which suffered flooding and violent storms. It also destroyed the Peruvian anchovy harvest.

ALTERING CLIMATE

The effects of El Niño are felt much farther afield than the eastern Pacific. Land areas in the western Pacific are prone to typhoons, like the one that killed 6,000 in the Philippines in 1991. Australia, Africa, and Southeast Asia suffer from droughts, causing poor harvests. The tinder-dry conditions also contribute to the disastrous fires in the rain forests of Sumatra and Borneo that have destroyed wildlife and caused widespread pollution.

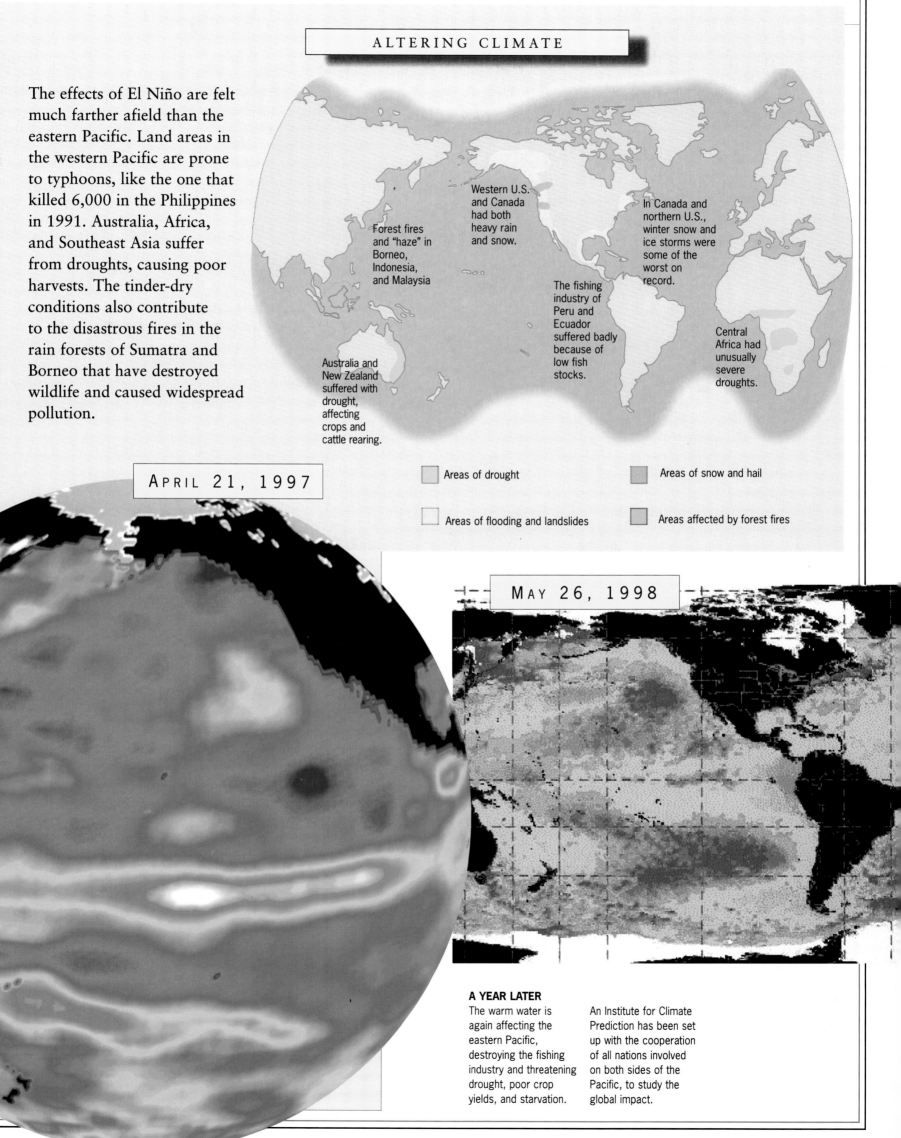

Forest fires and "haze" in Borneo, Indonesia, and Malaysia

Western U.S. and Canada had both heavy rain and snow.

In Canada and northern U.S., winter snow and ice storms were some of the worst on record.

The fishing industry of Peru and Ecuador suffered badly because of low fish stocks.

Central Africa had unusually severe droughts.

Australia and New Zealand suffered with drought, affecting crops and cattle rearing.

Areas of drought

Areas of flooding and landslides

Areas of snow and hail

Areas affected by forest fires

APRIL 21, 1997

MAY 26, 1998

A YEAR LATER

The warm water is again affecting the eastern Pacific, destroying the fishing industry and threatening drought, poor crop yields, and starvation.

An Institute for Climate Prediction has been set up with the cooperation of all nations involved on both sides of the Pacific, to study the global impact.

Seas and tides

See also:
- **Changing coasts** *p. 62*
- **Global weather** *p. 68*
- **Clouds and storms** *p. 70*

DEEP BLUE HOLES

The ocean can be divided into depth zones. Closest to land is the continental shelf (below), the flooded edges of the continent. This averages only 460 feet (140 m) or so at its deepest.

Beyond this, the continental slope drops away into the abyssal plain, the true ocean floor. This has an average depth of 12,000 feet (3,658 m). Some oceans have deep trenches. The deepest is the Mariana Trench in the western Pacific, which is over 36,000 feet (10,973 m) deep.

V ISIT A SEASHORE and you will see constant change. Twice a day, tides gradually creep up the beach, and then slowly retreat again.

Over a month (28 days), the tides alternate between the strong spring tides and the weaker neap tides, depending on the alignment of the sun, moon, and Earth.

Waves are created when the wind blows over the water surface, piling it up into ridges that then move in the direction of the wind. Big waves develop during storms and small ripples in calm weather.

BREAKERS ON THE SHORE

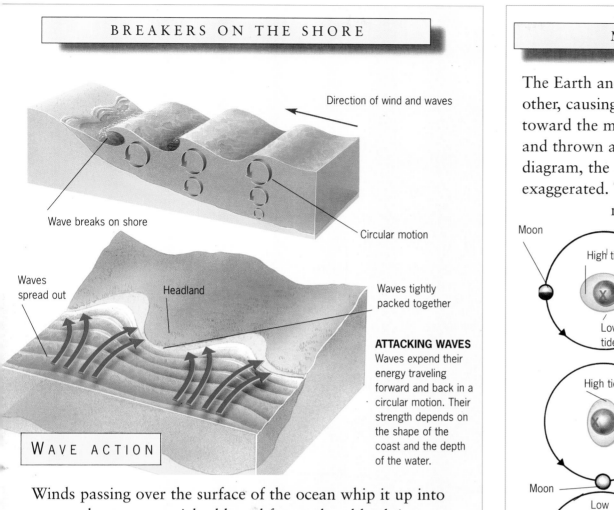

Direction of wind and waves

Wave breaks on shore

Circular motion

Waves spread out

Headland

Waves tightly packed together

WAVE ACTION

ATTACKING WAVES
Waves expend their energy traveling forward and back in a circular motion. Their strength depends on the shape of the coast and the depth of the water.

Winds passing over the surface of the ocean whip it up into waves, the water particles blasted forward and back in a circular motion. Although the water itself is only moving with this limited action, the wave disturbance can travel thousands of miles.

On reaching shallow water, the circular motion drags on the bottom and the wave topples over to form a breaker. When wave fronts approach land, they tend to curve around exposed headlands, attacking their cliffs from either side.

HIGH RISE AND FALL

The shape of the shoreline has an effect on the tides. The highest tidal range occurs where there are long bays and inlets, forcing the rising water into narrow gaps.

The Bay of Fundy, in Canada, (*see right*) has a tidal range of 50 feet (15 m) at the strong spring tides, when the sun and moon are exerting a pull together.

MOON POWER

The Earth and moon swing around each other, causing bulges of water (tides) dragged toward the moon on one side of the Earth, and thrown away from it on the other. In this diagram, the swing of the moon has been exaggerated. The harbor (see below) is marked x.

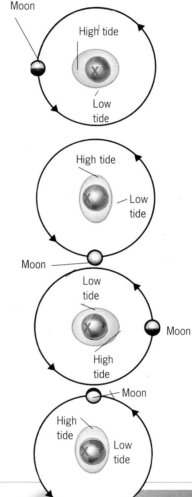

Moon — High tide — X — Low tide

SEPTEMBER 1
High tide at harbor X, because the moon directly overhead is pulling the water toward it.

High tide — Low tide — Moon

SEPTEMBER 8
Harbor X now has a low tide, because the moon has moved 90° around the Earth.

Low tide — X — High tide — Moon

SEPTEMBER 15
Harbor X has a high tide again, because a water bulge is being created by the Earth's movement around the moon.

Moon — High tide — Low tide

SEPTEMBER 22
Low tide again at harbor X, because it is midway between the tidal bulges once more.

Changing coasts

See also:
• **Eroding earth** p. 44 • **Seas and tides** p. 60
• **Ocean currents** p. 56

Below:
A Landsat compositional mosaic of the British Isles shows many examples of changing coastal scenery. Since the end of the Ice Age, the region has been gradually tilting, with northern Scotland rising out of the water and southern England slowly submerging.

RISING LAND
Around much of Scotland, the coastline has raised beaches—shelves of sand several feet above the present-day beach. These represent the level of the beaches during the Ice Age.

SCOTTISH FJORDS
On the west coast of Scotland, 400 million-year-old mountains are being attacked by the rough seas of the Atlantic, producing the typical eroded coastline of sea lochs and peninsulas.

SOUTHWEST BRITAIN
The estuaries of Devon and Cornwall are flooded river valleys, submerged over the last few thousand years.

THE BOUNDARY between the land and the sea is constantly changing. In some areas, the land is slowly being pounded and worn away by the action of the sea; elsewhere, the sea deposits sand and shingle along the shore, gradually building the coastline.

This results in two types of coastline. An eroded coast, such as the Scottish west coast, is admired for its rugged grandeur. A coast where material is deposited provides vacationers with sandy beaches.

HARD ROCKS, SOFT ROCKS

Mountain ranges jutting out into the sea are constantly broken down and eroded by the perpetual pounding of the waves. Such a coastline is jagged, with many headlands and inlets.

The material broken away from the land on an eroded coast often ends up on another coast that is slowly being built up. The broken rocky material from one area is slowly reduced to sand and shingle by the action of the sea. It is then spread by the action of the waves along beaches where the land is flatter. From the sky, a coastline that is gradually being built up has a smooth margin, often swept into spits and sand-bars by the prevailing sea currents.

THE NORTH SEA
Wave action is eroding the coast of Holderness. In East Anglia, sand and silt are being deposited, so adding to the coastline.

FORCES AT WORK

Along a coast that is being built up, rather than eroded, the sand and shingle are constantly on the move. Waves strike the coast at an angle, and wash the sand in a diagonal path up the beach. Some of this sand is washed straight back down in the backwash, and the next wave washes it up again at an angle. In this way, sand and shingle gather in a zigzag path along the beach. This process is known as beach drift, or longshore drift.

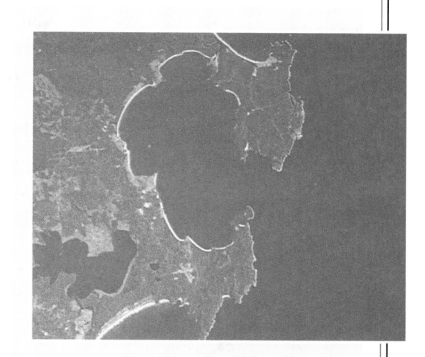

Swash

Direction of wind and waves

Backwash

BEACH MOVEMENT

TWO HEADS OR A LONG NOSE

When beach drift meets an inlet, the sand builds a sandbar across the mouth, forming a shallow lagoon. If it is across a river mouth, it will form a half bar, or spit.

When beach drift reaches a headland, it builds the sand out into the sea as a spit. Sometimes the spit reaches as far as an island and so joins the island to the mainland. This is called a tombolo. Jervis Bay in Australia is flanked by two tombolos.

WINDMILLS AND WATER

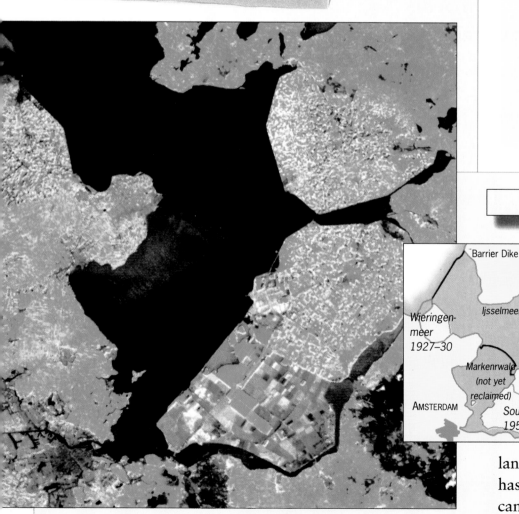

Barrier Dike

Ijsselmeer

Northeast polder 1937–50

Wieringen-meer 1927–30

Markenrwald (not yet reclaimed)

East Flevoland 1950–57

AMSTERDAM

South Flevoland 1959–68

The Dutch have altered their coastline since the seventh century. The shallow inlets of the Netherlands have been gradually walled off into "polders" and pumped out to provide farmland—3,000 square miles (7,770 sq km) in the past 800 years. Water in this land, some of it 16 feet (5 m) below sea level, has to be constantly drained using ditches, canals, pumps, and traditional windmills.

Coral islands

See also:
- **Volcano!** *p. 20*
- **Spreading rifts** *p. 22*
- **Rivers** *p. 38*
- **...and deltas** *p. 42*

RAIATEA
The single narrow fringing reef that surrounds both Raiatea and Tahaa can clearly be seen.

Below:
The Society Islands in French Polynesia display all the types of coral growth. They stretch from the southeast to the northwest. Those in the southeast (top left) are the youngest.

CORALS ARE TINY ORGANISMS. Ranging in size from one-tenth of an inch (2.5 mm) to several inches, they are found in shallow tropical seas. Corals live in large colonies, in limestone cups. As each one dies, a new one grows on top of its skeleton. Over thousands of years, they construct huge masses of limestone, called reefs. The Great Barrier Reef extends along the northeast coast of Australia for 1,250 miles (2,011 km).

These reefs provide a haven for all kinds of marine wildlife. Unfortunately, corals are very delicate and are very vulnerable to the effects of tourism, commercial fishing, and environmental pollution.

BORA-BORA
This is a classic island with a barrier reef that is hundreds of thousands of years older than its two sister islands (left). It has a well-developed barrier reef on all sides, as well as broad reef flats.

TAHAA
This island has subsided slightly more than her sister Raiatea and so has a barrier reef offshore. Both islands have high volcanic valleys with steeply eroded and wooded sides that end in a thin strip of beach.

THE LIFE AND DEATH OF A CORAL ISLAND

When an island is formed by volcanic action, coral builds around the coast, forming a fringing reef. Later, the island may sink and become smaller as the seafloor subsides. The reef continues to grow upward, separated from the shrinking island by a lagoon, forming a barrier reef. When the island sinks completely, because the seafloor has subsided, the coral is left forming a ring-shaped reef called an atoll.

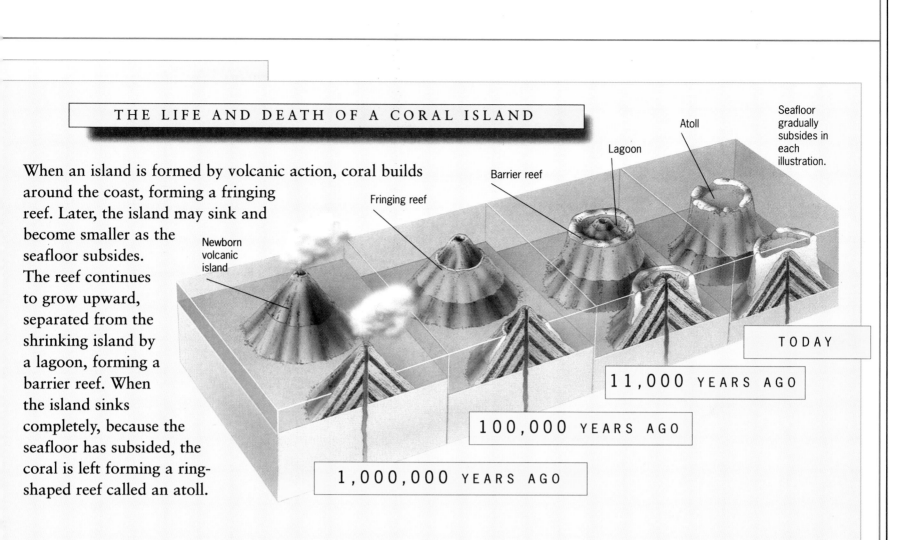

Seafloor gradually subsides in each illustration.

Atoll

Lagoon

Barrier reef

Fringing reef

Newborn volcanic island

TODAY

11,000 YEARS AGO

100,000 YEARS AGO

1,000,000 YEARS AGO

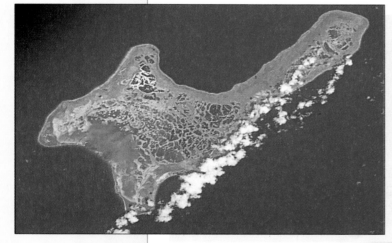

THE WORLDS BIGGEST ATOLL

Kiritimati is the largest atoll in the Pacific Ocean. Previously known as Christmas Island, it was discovered by Captain Cook on Christmas Eve in 1777.

Because of its remote position and barrenness, it was used as a testing site for nuclear weapons in the 1950s and 1960s.

TUPAI

This is the oldest of the islands shown. The central island has completely submerged, leaving a series of sub-merged reefs and lagoons, called an atoll. There are only three gaps in the reef.

Right:
A typical view of a Pacific coral island. The sea is shallow and exceptionally clear, with the reef growing only a short distance below the surface of the water.

PART THREE

Unseen forces

Under the sea, on land, and in the air, hidden forces are slowly altering the balance of our living planet.

Global weather

See also:
- **The air around us** p. 14
- **Ocean currents** p. 56
- **El Niño** p. 58
- **Clouds and storms** p. 70

FAST LANES IN THE SKY

High in the atmosphere, there is a mysterious system of very fast winds. These are the jet streams, a tubelike core of very fast winds that encircles the Earth. The jet stream is 186–300 miles (300–482 km) wide and 1–2 miles (2–3 km) deep. The winds blow eastward at speeds of up to 250 miles per hour (402 kph). Eastbound airliners use jet streams to save on time and fuel.

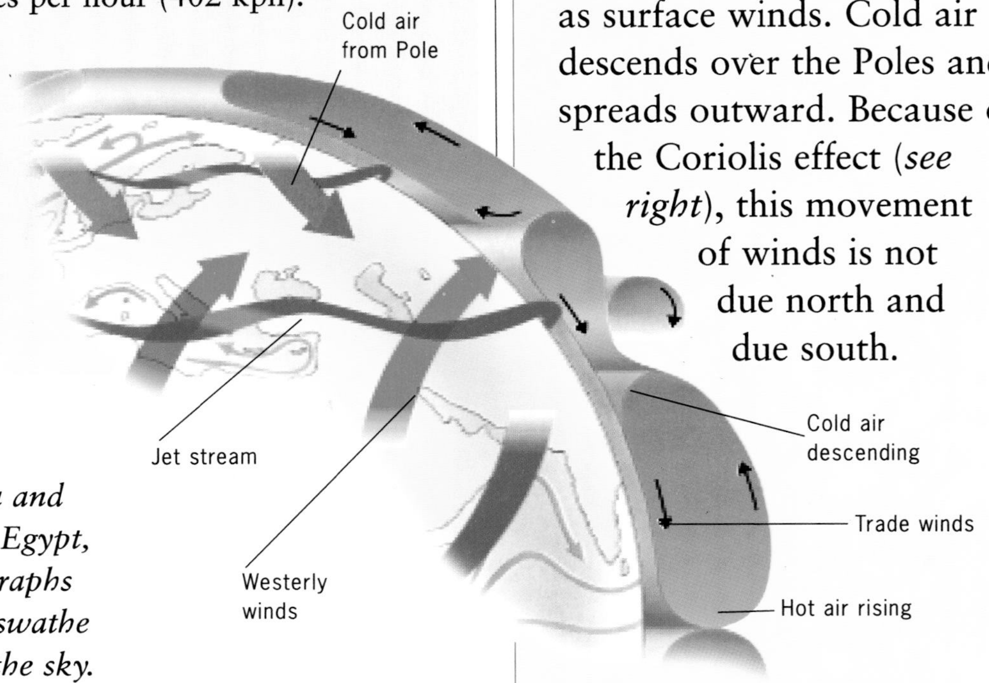

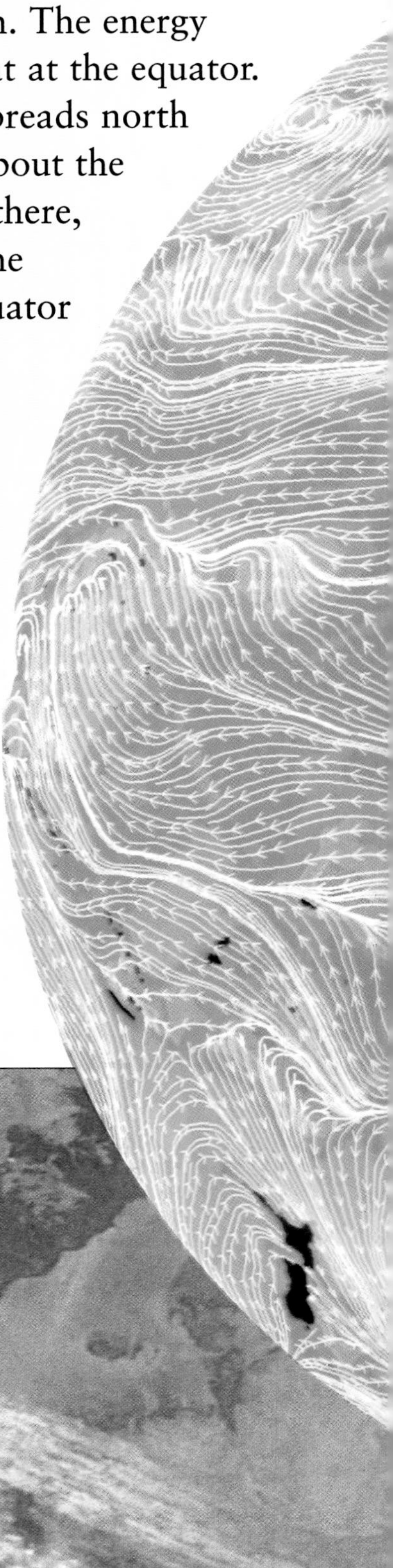

Below:
Over the Red Sea and the Nile River in Egypt, a satellite photographs a jet stream as a swathe of clouds across the sky.

Cold air from Pole

Jet stream

Westerly winds

Cold air descending

Trade winds

Hot air rising

OUR WEATHER is the result of the movement of winds across the Earth. The energy from the sun produces the heat at the equator. Hot air rises at the equator, spreads north and south, then descends at about the latitude of the Tropics. From there, the warm air spreads out to the Poles and also back to the equator as surface winds. Cold air descends over the Poles and spreads outward. Because of the Coriolis effect (*see right*), this movement of winds is not due north and due south.

"...TURN, TURN"

As the Earth spins on its axis, the equator moves faster than anywhere else, because the Earth is widest there, and so has farther to travel in 24 hours.

Anything—wind or an airplane—moving toward the equator is traveling over land that is moving eastward faster and faster, and so it finds itself lagging behind—it is deflected to the west. Likewise, anything that sets off due north or south from the equator is deflected to the east. This is called the Coriolis effect.

Rotation of the Earth

Actual path of trade winds

Equator

Theoretical path of trade winds

SWIRLING WIND
Surface winds over the Pacific Ocean. The arrows show in which direction the winds are blowing.

Right:
Winds sucked into a depression move into a spiral pattern because of the Coriolis effect. Moving away from the equator, they are deflected eastward; moving toward the equator, they are deflected westward.

Clouds and storms :

See also:

The air around us *p. 14*   • **El Niño** *p. 58*
Ocean currents *p. 56*   • **Killer winds** *p. 72*

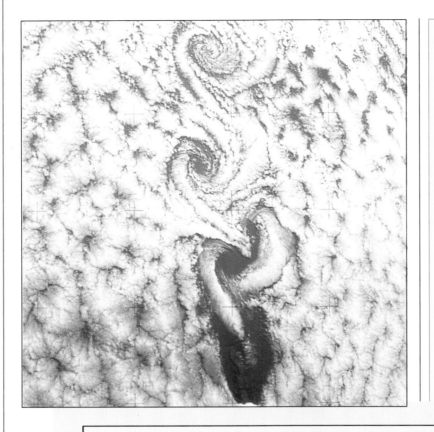

WATER, WHICH is essential for life on Earth, exists in three forms. Depending on temperature and air pressure, water can exist as a liquid, as a solid (ice), or as a gas (vapor).

Clouds are formed when water vapor in the air condenses into tiny droplets of water. In warm clouds, swirling air currents make the droplets collide and join together into larger droplets, which eventually fall as rain. These are the white fluffy cumulus clouds, or the low, gray stratus clouds.

If the cloud has a temperature below freezing, the water vapor turns into ice crystals. These high cirrus clouds look quite different—more feathery and wispy—from the fluffy cumulus.

THE PATTERNS IN THE SKY SHOW

Above and below: *Cloud patterns formed by wind show how, like water, wind flows around an obstruction. In Western Australia, clouds have formed over peaks of the Chichester range. These "pointed" clouds are rare.*

We are all familiar with the appearance of clouds as seen from below—the dark underbelly of storm clouds or the high, wispy mare's tails that suggest a change of weather is on the way. Clouds look even more spectacular from above, their shapes depending on whether there is land or sea below them.

Left: *When wind blows over a flat hillcrest, wave-like wind currents can build up clouds downwind of the obstacle. These cloud waves were photographed over South Australia.*

THE SOUND AND LIGHT SHOW

Thunderclouds form in warm, rapidly rising, moist air. As it rises, the moisture condenses, forming towering cumulonimbus clouds. Air circulation is so strong in these clouds that the raindrops cannot fall but just become bigger and more unstable. Eventually, they break apart, releasing an electric charge.

This electricity discharged to the ground forms a lightning flash, while the air expands with a crack of thunder.

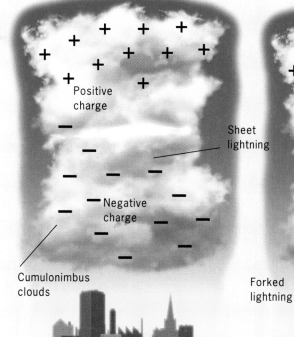

Positive charge

Sheet lightning

Negative charge

Cumulonimbus clouds

Positive charge

Negative charge

Forked lightning

Positive charge

Above and right:
A tropical storm above Brazil shows off its icy "anvil" head while forked lightning hits a desert in southern Arizona.

Killer winds

See also:
- **The air around us** *p. 14*
- **Ocean currents** *p. 56*
- **Global weather** *p. 68*
- **Clouds and storms** *p. 70*

AUGUST 25, 1992 19:00 HRS UTC
"ANDREW" APPROACHES LOUISIANA

THE TWO most powerful storms known to man are hurricanes and tornadoes. Both can wreak havoc on an almost unimaginable scale v seconds and with little warning.

THE COILED SERPENT

Hurricanes are formed in hot climates, when areas of low atmospheric pressure form over tropical oceans.

Large amounts of moisture evaporate, and as the hot air rises, more air is drawn in at sea level with great force. The wind blows inward and upward counterclockwise (clockwise in the southern hemisphere) around a central "eye," to produce the hurricane effect.

Those formed at low latitudes are called tropical cyclones or typhoons, as well as hurricanes, depending on where they occur in the world.

Above and right:
In August 1992, Hurricane Andrew caused the most damage and highest death toll of any hurricane in living memory. Between August 23 and August 27, it was responsible for 52 deaths and $22 billion in damage in the Bahamas, Louisiana, and Florida. (see below).

AUGUST 26, 1992 UTC
"ANDREW" HITS THE COAST

HOW HURRICANES FORM

Winds flowing outward

Eye of storm

Winds turn clockwise

Strong upcurrents

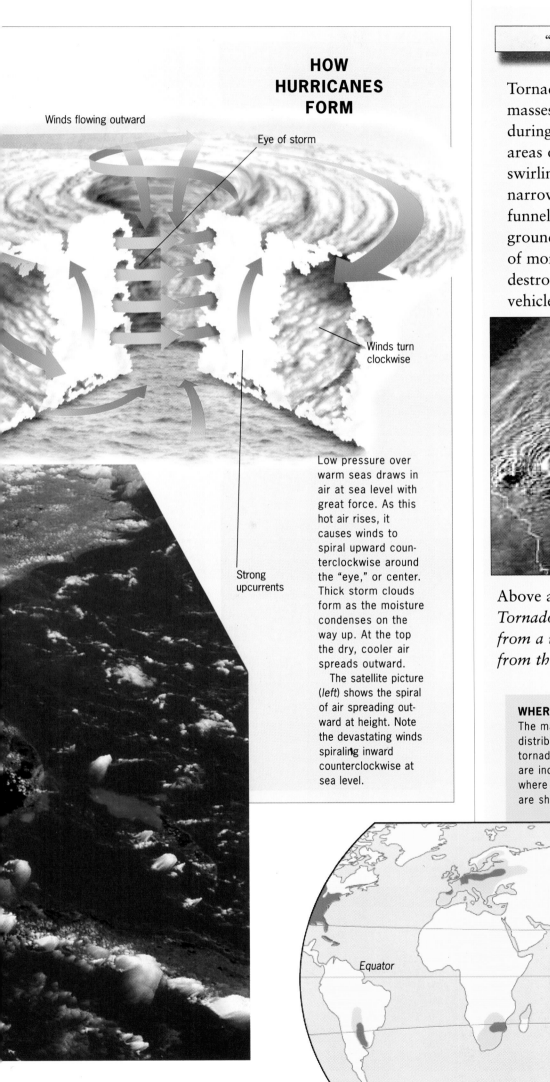

Low pressure over warm seas draws in air at sea level with great force. As this hot air rises, it causes winds to spiral upward counterclockwise around the "eye," or center. Thick storm clouds form as the moisture condenses on the way up. At the top the dry, cooler air spreads outward.

The satellite picture (*left*) shows the spiral of air spreading outward at height. Note the devastating winds spiraling inward counterclockwise at sea level.

"LET'S TWIST AGAIN…"

"LET'S TWIST AGAIN…"

Tornadoes are formed when hot and cold air masses meet and shear past each other during a thunderstorm. This causes small areas of intense low pressure that bring air swirling inward counterclockwise in a narrow column to form the tornado. The funnel-shaped cloud quickly extends to the ground and then swirls across land at speeds of more than 100 miles per hour (161 kph). It destroys buildings, sucks up people and vehicles, and flattens everything in its path.

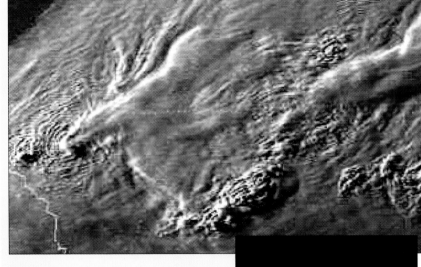

Above and right:
Tornadoes seen over Texas from a weather satellite and from the ground.

WHERE THE WINDS CAN KILL
The map below shows the distribution of hurricanes and tornadoes. Areas of intense storms are indicated in red; those areas where severe storms are less likely are shaded pink.

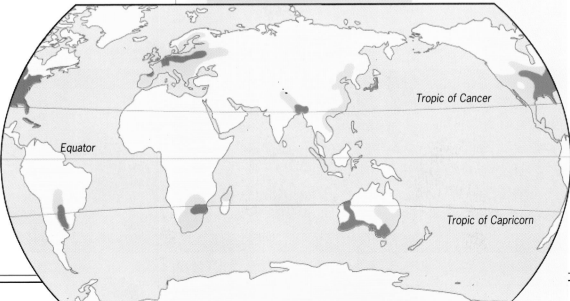

Tropic of Cancer

Equator

Tropic of Capricorn

Marks of humankind

See also:
- **Squashed forests** *p. 32*
- **Black gold** *p. 34*
- **Shifting deserts** *p. 46*
- **Moving bands** *p. 54*

Humans have put their impression on many parts of the Earth's surface—some of it for good and some for more misguided reasons. The effects, whatever the cause, are plain to see, and from space may be even more evident.

The Great Wall of China can be easily recognized from an orbiting spacecraft. Trackways can be traced in the desert and ruined cities plotted in rain forest mountains. The remote sensing equipment of satellites can shed light on an ancient past as easily as observing the progress of a modern war.

At night, our planet shimmers with light, like fireflies hovering in the sky on a warm summer evening.

Above:
This computer-enhanced view of our globe without cloud cover shows the intensity of lights from the cities of Europe, the Middle East, and the Indian subcontinent compared with that from the sparsely developed continent of Africa.

Right:
In the middle of Siberian Russia lies Omsk, a city built astride the track of the Trans-Siberian Railway. Drifting snow and a low camera angle accentuate the gridlike pattern of the city in the "middle of nowhere."

NATURAL AND MANMADE BOUNDARIES

The boundaries between different nations often can be appreciated better from space than from the ground. Where there are political as well as natural boundaries, it is even more evident. Often, political boundaries lie along geographical features like rivers.

Parana River

The Itaipú Dam Project is a joint Brazil-Paraguay hydroelectric power scheme—the largest in the world. The dam at the bottom of the reservoir is 6 miles (10 km) long and 200 feet (61 m) high. Its output is about 12,600 megawatts.

The boundary between Brazil (right) and Argentina is marked by farm fields on the Brazilian side and managed forest between the Argentinian border and the river.

Iguagu Falls

The Iguagu River forms a natural boundary with the Parana River, and they encompass two sides of a national park. Within its boundaries lie the spectacular *Cataratas del Iguagu*, or Iguagu Falls, which plunge down 270 feet (82 m) into a steep canyon.

THE BRAZIL-ARGENTINA BORDER

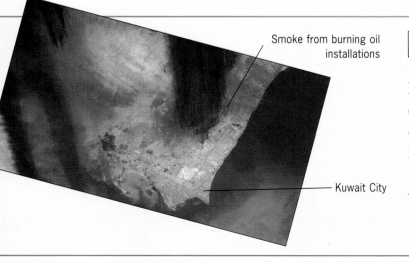

Smoke from burning oil installations

Kuwait City

WAR FROM THE AIR

Imaging from a remote sensor can track a tank in a desert or a platoon on a tundra. Similarly, a plume of oil smoke was tracked as soon as Saddam Hussein had ignited the oil wells (left) in his retreat from Kuwait in 1991. Scientists could analyze the clouds, determine their chemical makeup, and warn of potential problems.

Holes in the sky

See also:
- **The air around us** p. 14
- **El Niño** p. 58
- **Global weather** p. 68
- **Clouds and storms** p. 70

A THINNING SHIELD

There is a layer in the atmosphere, 7–31 miles (11–50 km) above the Earth, that is rich in a kind of oxygen called ozone. This layer is important because it filters out much of the ultraviolet (UV) radiation from the sun.

Since the mid-1980s, scientists have found that there is an annual thinning of this ozone layer, particularly over the Poles. The most obvious cause seems to be pollution by chemicals, particularly chlorofluorocarbons (CFCs). Sunlight breaks down the CFCs in the atmosphere, and the released chlorine reduces the filtering properties of the ozone. The increase in UV radiation that reaches us can lead to skin cancers.

THE EARTH'S climate is constantly changing. We need only look at the strata of ancient rocks, or the ice layers in Greenland, to tell that. Gases from volcanoes and hot springs continually change the composition of the atmosphere. But there is a mass of evidence to suggest that the climate is now changing much faster than normal. The agent of this change is ourselves. Industry and technology fill the atmosphere with pollutants, while chemical wastes are altering the physics and chemistry of the atmosphere itself. These changes are bound to affect our lives.

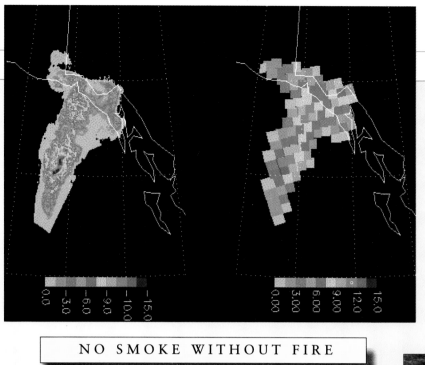

NO SMOKE WITHOUT FIRE

Erupting volcanoes, such as Mount Pinatubo and Mount St. Helens, belch out immense quantities of gas, dust, and ash into the atmosphere. Vehicles, power stations, and factories further pollute the atmosphere by releasing sulfur dioxide and nitrogen oxide. These pollutants can be carried great distances by the winds and are removed only by rain or snow.

Some of the chemicals released can dissolve in rainwater, forming a corrosive kind of rain known as "acid rain." This has had the effect of rotting crops, poisoning lakes, killing trees, and causing respiratory diseases.

THAT SINKING FEELING

Over the last 200 years or so, there has been a change in the atmosphere. Industry has generated carbon dioxide from the burning of fossil fuels, and other increased gases include methane and water vapor. All these together produce the "greenhouse effect."

These gases allow the sun's rays to reach the Earth's surface, but the heat radiated from the surface is then trapped by the gases, thus increasing its temperature. On a worldwide scale, this may produce global warming. One effect would be to melt the ice caps and raise the sea level. Low-lying areas such as Florida (*left*) would be very vulnerable to this.

AN EL NIÑO SIDESHOW

Early 1998 saw devastating fires in Borneo for the second year running, the result of "slash and burn" agriculture, in which areas of natural forest are burned to provide farming land. A simultaneous drought, as a result of the "El Niño effect," meant that the fires raged out of control. Satellite sensors showed the rise and fall of the atmospheric haze in Southeast Asia over three months that caused severe health problems.

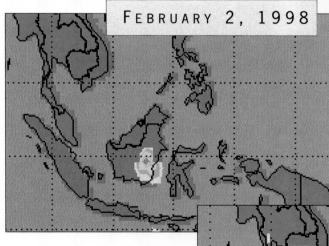

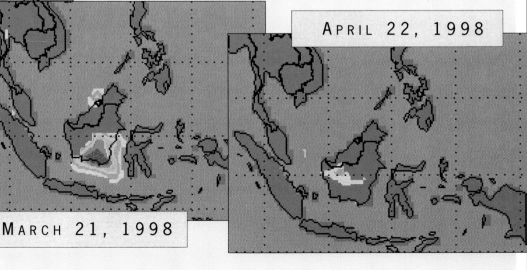

Left:
The hole in the ozone layer was first detected by the British Antarctic Survey at Halley Bay in Antarctica in 1982. This first satellite image was taken in 1988 by NASA's satellite TOMS. Since then, the hole has been enlarging.

Soiled waters

See also:
- **The air around us** p. 14
- **El Niño** p. 58
- **Global weather** p. 68
- **Clouds and storms** p. 70

Below:
Madagascar is running out of soil, because it is being washed into the sea. The red stain in the water shows clearly in this shot from the space shuttle of the Betsiboka River outfall, with the Mozambique Channel at the top.

THE OCEAN has always been regarded as having an infinite capacity—a dustbin that could absorb anything, however much rubbish was dumped into it.

Sadly, this has proved not to be true. The enormous volume of human garbage and industrial waste built up over the centuries is now altering the composition and quality of the sea.

The problem is most obvious in confined seas with poor circulation, such as the Mediterranean, and in areas bordering on busy ports and large cities. But recently, fears have also been expressed about the condition of even the deepest parts of the ocean floor.

A SPILL TOO MANY

Much of the world's economy is based on oil, which has to be transported by tanker from place to place. During the Arab-Israeli War in the 1960s, a new generation of "supertankers" was built to enable oil traffic to bypass the Suez Canal. The first big accident involving an oil supertanker was the oil spill from the *Torrey Canyon* off Cornwall, England, in 1967.

Right:
On March 24, 1989, the tanker Exxon Valdez *ran aground in Alaska, rupturing her tanks and spilling out crude oil. The oil slick that resulted polluted the shoreline, took years to clean up, and cost millions.*

Below:
The Straits of Hormuz, at the southern end of the Persian Gulf, sees 20 percent of the world's oil traffic pass through its waters. Oil slicks, debris, and waste discharges are all killing its marine environment.

Top:
Tanker spills are spectacular, but most pollution comes from the discharge of machine waste. The wildlife suffers just the same.

BUSY CROSSROADS

The nature of sea traffic means that some areas are much busier than others. The English Channel, the Cape of Good Hope, the Malay Straits, and the Straits of Hormuz are some of the busier waterways in the world, and are, therefore, the most vulnerable.

International agencies, such as the Intergovernmental Maritime Organization, have been set up to minimize human impact on such areas by regulating sea traffic and advising on tanker design.

PART FOUR

Snapshots of our world

Fly by Earth—four global views show us how we look from space.

The Americas and the Eastern Pacific

THE TOPOGRAPHY of the Americas is one of the most varied to be found on this planet.

The northern parts of Canada lie in the Arctic, while the southern tip of South America was, until recently (in geological time), joined to Antarctica.

North and Central America

North America occupies the northern part of the western hemisphere and has a core of ancient rock known as the Canadian Shield.

Huge mountain chains run down the eastern and western flanks of North America. The oldest are the Appalachian Mountains in the east, formed some 400 million years ago. They have been worn away by

The Amazon River stretches for 3,997 miles (6,437 km). It is the world's second longest river, surrounded by some of the most dense equatorial rain forest in the world. It is also the most threatened.

DEATH VALLEY, California, is the lowest part of the American continent. Although the valley rises to over 10,000 feet (3,048 m) in places, the lowest point is 282 feet (86 m) below sea level.

wind and rain for so long that they are now much lower than the younger, sharp-crested Rocky Mountains to the west. Between lie the Great Plains—originally home to more than 500 tribes of Native Americans, who were gradually ousted by immigrant white settlers. North America is rich in minerals and oil.

Central America, the thin ribbon of land that joins the continents, encompasses more than 30 countries and many small islands with mountainous, volcanic landscapes.

South America

The world's fourth largest continent straddles the equator and includes one of its richest resources— the Amazon rain forest. This mass of virgin forest is a major source of the world's oxygen and contains almost half of all the world's living

LAKE SUPERIOR is the second largest lake in the world and the biggest of the Great Lakes. These lakes were formed at the end of the Ice Age, when melting ice filled ground-out hollows.

species. The Amazon itself contains more than one-fifth of the world's freshwater.

The Andes mountains run down the western seaboard of South America.

STAGGERING STATISTICS

1 **Highest point**
Aconcagua, Argentina 22,833 feet
(6,960 m)

2 **Lowest point**
Death Valley, California 282 feet
(86 m) below sea level

3 **Largest lake**
Lake Superior, Canada/U.S.
32,140 square miles (83,243 sq km)

4 **Longest river**
Amazon, Brazil 3,997 miles (6,437 km)

CANADA

USA

HAWAII

GALÁPAGOS
ISLANDS

BRAZIL

FRENCH
POLYNESIA

ARGENTINA

DEEP INSIDE the Andes stands the snow-shrouded peak of Aconcagua. This extinct volcano is South America's highest mountain.

Europe and Africa

Caspian Sea, and Aral Sea.

Europe
Europe is the second smallest continent in the world, but it has a complicated layout and an ancient geological history.

It stretches from the Ural Mountains in the east, where it joined onto Asia some 300 million years ago, to the Atlantic shoreline. To the north are the mountains of Scotland and Norway, which are about 400 million years old. To the south are crumpled fold mountains that are still forming as Europe and Africa slowly slide past one another—the Atlas Mountains in the north of Africa, then Sicily, the Apennines, the Alps, and the Carpathians.

STAGGERING STATISTICS

1   **Highest point in Africa**
Kilimanjaro, Tanzania 19,341 feet (5,895 m)

2   **Highest point in Europe**
Mount Elbrus, Caucasus 18,511 feet (5,642 m)

3   **Lowest point**
Lake Assal, Djibouti 515 feet (157 m) below sea level

4   **Longest river (in the world)**
Nile, Egypt 4,130 miles (6,650 km)

THE NORTH and south continental landmasses were once separated by the mighty Tethys Ocean. That ocean has almost disappeared as Africa has slowly moved northeast toward Europe, squeezing and crumpling the mountains in between, and leaving only the "puddles" of the Mediterranean, Black Sea,

THE NORTH-ERNMOST part of Europe lies inside the Arctic Circle, where the conifer forests of Norway, Sweden, and Finland give way to icy plains.
  The whole of Scandinavia was covered with glaciers during the last Ice Age, and the land, relieved of the great weight of ice, is still rising.

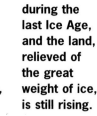

The movement of Africa is slowly stretching Europe in an east-west direction, producing the rift valleys of the Rhône and the Rhine, and the North Sea oil fields. The complex arrangement of bays, lochs, peninsulas, fjords, and inlets gives Europe the longest coastline of any continent.

The climate is also complex, ranging from the balmy Mediterranean in the south, to the northern areas where the warm westerlies met the cold polar easterlies, creating unstable weather conditions. Eastern Europe, far from the sea, has a continental climate, with very hot summers and very cold winters.

Africa

Africa is about three times the size of Europe and is built around chunks of ancient metamorphic rock. A system of rift valleys runs up the eastern side of the continent, marking a line where the continent will one day tear itself apart.

Madagascar has already broken away, and one day East Africa may also become an island. The Great Rift Valley system continues up East Africa into Ethiopia and the Red Sea. This rift valley, formed over some five million years, is where mankind first evolved some two million years ago, spreading out to colonize the world.

Like two pieces of a jigsaw, the west coast of Africa reflects the eastern coast of South America, to which it was once joined.

Africa is crossed by the equator, marked by tropical rainforest. On either side lies tropical grassland, and beyond that are belts of desert—the Sahara in the north and the Kalahari in the south. The extreme north and south have a Mediterranean climate.

THIS FALSE color Landsat image shows the Nile River with its delta, as well as Sinai and the Red Sea.
  The Red Sea is slowly widening as part of the Rift Valley system. In time, it will link up with the Mediterranean, but not for many millions of years.

Asia, Australia, and the Western Pacific

THESE THREE vast areas, including two continents, cover half the globe.

Asia

Asia is the largest continent in the world, accounting for about one-third of the total land surface of the Earth. The islands of the East Indies stretch below the equator, while the northern tip of Siberia lies within the Arctic Circle.

In the west, Asia has been joined to Europe along the Ural Mountains for some 300 million years. In the east, it narrows to a point at the Bering Strait only 53 miles (85 km) from North America.

In the south, it is almost joined to Africa, but the Red Sea is gradually widening, pushing the two continents apart.

The highest mountains in the world—the Himalayas —were formed a mere 50 million years ago, when the Indian plate moved northward and collided with the Eurasian plate, forcing the younger rocks upward. That movement is still taking place. The plate movement also crumpled up rocks to form the islands of the East Indies.

Along the eastern coast, the Pacific Ocean floor is slowly being drawn down under the continent, resulting in the islands of Japan, the Philippines, the Kurile islands, and the Aleutians.

THE TIBETAN plateau behind the Himalayas is a windswept place. What agriculture is attempted there exists in river valleys such as the Yarlung Zangbo Jiang, where winter wheat and barley are grown.

Australia

Australia is the largest island continent in the world. It was once joined to Antarctica but broke off some 60 million years ago and drifted northward. It is still moving north, and eventually it will collide with Asia.

Australia lies across the Tropic of Capricorn, hence its interior is desert and tropical grassland. The north has equatorial rain forest, while the south has a Mediterranean climate.

The east of Australia has a chain of mountains running north to south, known as the Great Dividing Range. Most of the population lives in the coastal strip between these

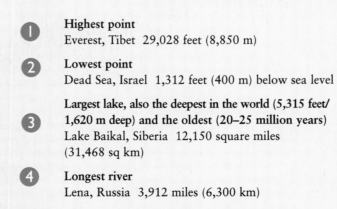

STAGGERING STATISTICS

1. **Highest point**
   Everest, Tibet 29,028 feet (8,850 m)

2. **Lowest point**
   Dead Sea, Israel 1,312 feet (400 m) below sea level

3. **Largest lake, also the deepest in the world (5,315 feet/ 1,620 m deep) and the oldest (20–25 million years)**
   Lake Baikal, Siberia 12,150 square miles (31,468 sq km)

4. **Longest river**
   Lena, Russia 3,912 miles (6,300 km)

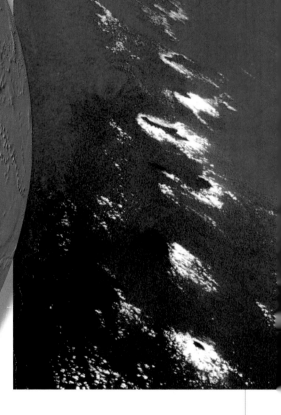

THE PACIFIC Ocean is littered with volcanic activity. This string of volcanic cones, outlined with cloud, is in Java, just north of Australia. Many of these volcanoes are still active.

THE KURILE Islands between Russia and Japan form part of the "Ring of Fire." Just west of these islands, the seafloor plunges to its greatest depths on Earth.

mountains and the sea. The only other notable range—the Olgas—lies in the center of Australia and includes the famous Uluru, or Ayers Rock.

Western Pacific

The volcanic islands of the Western Pacific form arcs from the Aleutian Islands and Japan to the Philippines and New Guinea, following the deep ocean trenches. Many of these volcanoes are still active, and form the famous "Ring of Fire."

A further series of volcanic island chains runs from New Guinea to Fiji. These are the remains of hotspot volcanoes.

This area is known as Melanesia. It was first colonized some 30,000 years ago by hunters from Southeast Asia—the same aborigines who first colonized Australia.

The North and South Poles

THE POLAR REGIONS are the coldest places on Earth. Within the Arctic and Antarctic Circles are areas that sometimes get no sunlight at all, and other places where in summer the sun never sets. The poles themselves experience six months of darkness followed by six months of daylight.

The North Pole
The North Pole lies in the Arctic Ocean. The ice cap floats in the ocean with pack ice and only a few scattered islands lying beneath it. The only land-mass of any size is Green-land, which also has an ice cap. Glaciers along the coast produce thousands of icebergs every year. These icebergs travel south to Newfoundland in the Labrador Current and are eventually melted by the Gulf Stream.

The North Pole, although so far from industrialized nations, suffers from pollution. DDT has been found in cod in the Barents Sea, and Caesium 137 from Chernobyl was found in northern Scandi-navia.

The South Pole
At the South Pole lies the continent of Antarctica, twice the size of Australia. It is a typical continent

with an old landmass at the center and mountain ranges along the edges. Most of the landmass is covered in ice, and the

weight is so great that it presses down the interior below sea level. Only about one percent of the

Antarctic is free from ice, consisting mainly of mountains that protrude through it.

The few parts of the

GREENLAND IS almost totally covered by an ice cap. If the ice were to melt, the land on which it rested would rise by about 3 feet (1 m).

coastal plain that are free from ice are cold and barren. However, the summer sunlight produces blooms of algae in the sea that attract vast shoals of fish. These fish, in their turn, are hunted by seals and flocks of penguins.

There are even active volcanoes in the Antarctic, including Mount Erebus, the most southerly active volcano in the world.

THE NORTH POLAR REGIONS

THE SOUTH
Pole is
almost totally
covered with
ice, account-
ing for 90
percent of
the Earth's
freshwater
reserves.
This massive
ice sheet is
6,560 feet
(2,000 m)
thick on
average.

STAGGERING STATISTICS

 Thickness of Antarctic ice sheet
about 6,560 feet (2,000 m) on average

Area of Antarctic ice sheet
5,000 million square miles (13,000 million sq km)

Area of Greenland ice sheet
669,710 square miles (1,734,550 sq km)

Deepest point below Arctic ice
Pole Abyssal Plain 18,052 feet (5,502 m)

Glossary

A

Abyssal plain
The flat bed of the ocean between the *continents*, from which the *ocean ridges* rise and which dips into *ocean trenches*. The abyssal plain is between 11,499 and 18,199 feet (3,505 and 5,547 m) deep and lies in permanent darkness.

Acid rain
Rain that has become acidic because of chemicals dissolved from the atmosphere. A common cause of acid rain is waste gases given off by factories that can damage crops and poison *groundwater* downwind from the source of pollution. Acid rain is also caused naturally by the gases erupted from *volcanoes*.

Alluvium
Loose material, such as sand, mud, or silt, that is deposited by rivers and streams. Some of the most fertile farmland is formed on alluvium deposited by rivers in flood.

Andesitic volcano
A *volcano* that erupts andesitic *lava*, which is relatively rich in the *mineral* silica. This makes the lava thick and easily solidified. Such volcanoes are formed through the action of *plate tectonics*, where one plate is overriding another. The *magma* is derived from molten plate material, and the eruptions tend to be very violent and explosive, in contrast to *basaltic volcanoes*.

Arctic Circle
The theoretical line, at a latitude of 66°30 North, within which the sun does not rise during at least one day of the year, and does not set during at least one day. Its equivalent in the southern hemisphere is the Antarctic Circle.

Asteroid
A body of rock, smaller than a planet or a moon, that orbits the sun in the solar system. Asteroids are sometimes called "planetoids."

Asthenosphere
A layer within the Earth's *mantle* that is fairly soft. It is the lubricating layer on which the Earth's plates move during the process of *plate tectonics*. The layer that comprises the plates is called the *lithosphere*.

Atoll
A ring-shaped *coral* reef. Atolls form when islands gradually subside, allowing any coral reef around the edge to grow, keeping pace with the rate of subsidence. The *lagoon* in the middle represents the original area of the island.

B

Basalt
A dark, fine-grained, *igneous rock*. It erupts from fissures in *volcanoes* that do not erupt explosively, and then cools and hardens. Basaltic *lava* is usually erupted at the bottom of the ocean. It can form lava fields thousands of feet thick.

Basaltic volcano
A *volcano* that erupts basaltic *lava*. Basaltic volcanoes are broad and flat because the lava tends to flow some distance and spread out before solidifying into *basalt* rock. These volcanoes are found where new plates are being generated. The *magma* is low in silica, derived from the *mantle*, and produces gentle eruptions.

Breaker
An ocean wave that curls over when it reaches shallow water and breaks into surf on the shore.

British Antarctic Survey
An institute of Britain's Natural Environment Research Council, specializing in the study of Antarctica.

C

Calcite
The mineral calcium carbonate ($CaCO_3$). It is easily broken down by the action of acid in rainwater. It is the principal ingredient of *limestone*, and its instability accounts for the characteristic erosion patterns of limestone landscapes.

Caldera
A very large *crater* caused by the inward collapse of a *volcano* into its *magma* chamber. If the volcano is extinct, the crater will be filled with water.

Canyon
A deep gorge cut in the rock by a stream. Canyons are often found in arid areas subjected to heavy flash floods at certain times of the year, such as the southwestern U.S.

Cavern
A cave, particularly one formed by solution in a *limestone* terrain.

Chlorofluorocarbon (CFC)
A gaseous substance, a compound of chlorine, fluorine, and carbon, used in many industrial processes. It is not easily broken down, and its buildup in the atmosphere can lead to pollution problems as it damages the *ozone layer*.

Cirque
An armchair-shaped hollow in the side of a mountain with a *glacier*. The cirque is the place where the glacier originates, the great weight of the accumulated snow and ice grinding out the hollow. Cirque is a French term,

originally applying to the Alps. In the Scottish Highlands the feature is called a corrie, and in the Welsh mountains a cwm.

Climate
The meteorological conditions of an area, averaged out over a long period of time. This differs from weather, in that weather is the day-to-day variation in the climate of an area.

Conglomerate
A coarse *sedimentary rock* consisting of rock fragments cemented together.

Coniferous
Description of a tree that bears its seeds in cones. Coniferous trees usually have leaves in the form of needles. Pine, fir, and spruce are typical coniferous trees.

Continent
A very large landmass.

Continental shelf
The submerged edge of a continent, covered by seawater to a depth of about 449 feet (137 m). Beyond this is the continental slope, where the sea becomes deeper very rapidly.

Convection
The process whereby a gas or liquid moves upward when it becomes warm and less dense, and the cooler, denser portion flows in to take its place.

Coral
A kind of tiny marine animal without a backbone. Corals are sedentary, extracting calcium carbonate from seawater to make limy shells. Hundreds of thousands of coral shells built up on each other form a reef.

Core
The innermost part of the Earth's structure. It is mostly

made of iron and consists of two parts—an inner core that is solid and an outer core that is liquid.

Coriolis effect
The process by which anything moving toward the *equator,* such as the wind, is deflected to the west, and anything moving away from the equator is deflected to the east. The effect is caused by the rotation of the Earth.

Crater
A circular depression formed at the top of an erupting *volcano.* It can also be caused by the impact of a *meteorite.*

Crevasse
A deep crack, especially in the surface of a glacier. The rigid surface of a *glacier* cracks and splits as the glacier flows round a sharp corner of its valley, or over a hump on the valley floor.

Crust
The topmost layer of the Earth's structure. It is made of the lightest rocky material and surrounds the *mantle.* Two types of crust are recognized—oceanic crust and continental crust. Oceanic crust is denser and forms the floors of the oceans. The continental crust is the only part of the Earth's structure we normally see, and it is lighter than the oceanic crust. Individual masses of the continental crust form the continents and are embedded in the oceanic crust. The plates that take part in *plate tectonics* consist of the crust and the topmost layer of the *mantle.*

Crystal
A naturally formed piece of a mineral that has a specific shape. This shape reflects the arrangement of atoms in the *mineral,* just as the rectangular shape of a house reflects the shape of the bricks.

D

Deciduous
Describes a tree that loses its leaves in the autumn and grows new ones in spring, for example the oak and the ash.

Delta
An area of *deposition* at the mouth of a river, where sandy material washed down by the river piles up as sandbanks, and the river has to cut its own channels through. A delta forms where there are no sea currents to wash the deposited material away.

Deposition
The process by which material washed along by a river or a stream settles on the bottom when the current slackens, to build up beds of *sediment.*

E

Ecosphere
The theoretical shell around the sun in which it is possible for life as we know it to exist. Inside the inner boundary of the ecosphere the heat and radiation from the sun would be too intense, while outside the outer boundary conditions are too cold.

Ejecta
The broken material thrown out by a *volcano* or blasted out by the impact of a *meteorite.*

El Niño
A pattern of weather caused by the disruption of the normal flow of the prevailing winds and ocean currents in the Pacific Ocean. It happens every few years, with disastrous effects.

Epicenter
The point on the Earth's surface directly above the focus of an earthquake. Normally the greatest damage is done there.

Equator
The theoretical line drawn around the Earth at latitude 0°.

Erosion
The breaking down of rocks and landforms by the natural processes of weather, by river currents, or by the pounding of waves.

F

Fjord
A long, deep, narrow inlet from the ocean, bounded by steep cliffs. Fjords are carved by the action of glaciers and are common on the west coast of Norway.

Fossil
The remains of a plant or animal found preserved in rocks. Most fossils are found in *sedimentary rock.*

G

Glacier
A mass of ice that builds up on land by repeated snowfalls and then moves slowly downhill under the influence of gravity.

Gondwana
The supercontinent that existed in the southern hemisphere up to about 50 million years ago. It was comprised of South America, Africa, India, Australia, and Antarctica. It gradually split up, and the *continents* slowly moved to their present positions.

Granite
An *igneous rock* consisting of large *crystals* and containing a high proportion of silica in the form of the *mineral* quartz.

Greenhouse effect
The warming of the Earth's surface due to the changing composition of the atmosphere, allowing the sun's rays in but preventing excess heat from being radiated out.

Grike
A joint in a slab of *limestone* widened by the effect of *erosion* and weathering.

Groundwater
Water found under the surface of the Earth. Much of the rain water that falls sinks into the ground, soaking the soil and accumulating at depth. At a certain depth, the soil and rocks become saturated with water and can hold no more. This is known as the zone of saturation, and the top level of this is known as the water table.

Gyre
A vast circular movement of ocean currents.

I

Ice Age
A time when the Earth's *climate* was cooler and the *ice sheets* and *glaciers* were more extensive than they are at present. The end of the last Ice Age was about 20,000 years ago.

Ice cap
A *glacier* that is not confined to a valley, but covers a large continental area. Such caps are found in Antarctica and Greenland, and also on the Arctic Ocean. Unlike valley glaciers, where the movement is downhill, the movement of an ice cap is outward as new ice accumulates from snowfalls in the center. The terms *ice cap* and *ice sheet* are often used interchangeably.

Ice sheet
A *glacier* that covers a wide area of land, rather than being confined in a valley.

Igneous rock
One of the three main kinds of rock that make up the Earth's crust. It is formed when hot molten material called *magma* cools and solidifies.

Glossary/2

Island arc
A string of volcanic islands in the shape of an arc, formed on the inside curve of an *ocean trench* through the action of *plate tectonics*.

J

Jet stream
A particularly strong wind found in the stratosphere in mid-latitudes, blowing eastward. It can reach speeds of 249 miles per hour (400 kph). It is a result of the circulation pattern of the atmosphere around the globe and is often sought out by long-distance airline pilots to assist their eastward passage.

K

Karst
A very dry landscape form found in a region of *limestone*. This rock dissolves easily on exposure, particularly through the effects of *acid rain*. Joints or cracks in the rock are dissolved into wide openings—*grikes*—leaving the intervening areas of rock as upstanding blocks called "clints." Karst is named after the area in the former Yugoslavia where the landform is common.

L

Lagoon
A shallow area of seawater partly or totally cut off from the sea by a barrier, such as a coral reef.

Lava
Molten rocky material produced when *magma* erupts from a *volcano*. It then cools and hardens on the Earth's surface. Basaltic lava is quite runny and flows for long distances before solidifying. Andesitic lava is stiff and easily solidified, and so does not flow very far.

Levee
A raised bank along the sides of a river, built up from sediment deposited during successive floods.

Limestone
A *sedimentary rock* consisting mostly of the mineral *calcite*.

Lithosphere
The outer shell of the Earth that forms the *tectonic* plates. It is comprised of the *crust* and the topmost section of the *mantle*. It is solid and moves about on the softer *asthenosphere* below.

Longshore drift
An effect of a sea current in which sand and pebbles are transported in one direction along a beach. The effect results in *sandbars*, sand spits, and *tombolos*.

M

Magma
Molten rock that exists below the surface of the Earth. It is composed largely of silicates with dissolved gases. When magma erupts at the surface through volcanic action, it becomes known as *lava*.

Mantle
The part of the Earth's structure that lies between the *core* and the *crust*. The mantle comprises the greatest proportion of the Earth's volume. It is made of a stony material and is solid, except for a soft layer close to the outside. This soft layer, called the "*asthenosphere*," provides the lubrication that allows the outermost part of the Earth to move about in the process of *plate tectonics*.

Marble
A *metamorphic rock* formed when *limestone* is subjected to heat and pressure.

Meander
A loop formed in a slow-moving river as it crosses a floodplain. As the river winds through sediments deposited on the valley floor, the current is always faster on the outside of the curves, eroding the bank away. On the inside of the curve, eroded material being carried along is deposited as a beach. In this way the curve of the river extends itself—a process known as meandering.

Mediterranean-type climate
A climate characterized by warm, wet westerly winds in winter and hot, dry summers. South Africa, southern Australia, parts of Chile, and California experience a Mediterranean climate as well as the Mediterranean countries.

Metamorphic rock
A rock that forms when a pre-existing rock is heated or crushed so much that its *mineral* content changes. In this process, it is important that the rock does not melt, otherwise the result would be an *igneous rock*.

Meteorite
A lump of rocky or metallic matter in space. Sometimes a meteorite will fall through the atmosphere and strike the Earth. The glowing trail produced by this fall is called a meteor.

Mineral
One of the constituents of a rock; a naturally formed substance that has a particular chemical composition. In their purest forms, minerals form *crystals*. A rock may be made up of a number of different minerals.

N

NASA
National Aeronautics and Space Administration, established by the United States in 1958 to administer space exploration.

Neap tide
The tidal condition that occurs twice a month when the gravitational influence of the sun and the moon are pulling at right angles to each other. During neap tides there is only a small tidal range, with the high tides being relatively low and the low tides relatively high. The opposite condition is the *spring tide*.

O

Ocean ridge
A ridge formed along the ocean floor by the upwelling of molten material from below the *crust*. This is where new plates are formed in the process of *plate tectonics*.

Ocean trench
Elongated depression in the ocean floor. It is formed by the process of *plate tectonics*, at the site where an old plate is destroyed as it slips down below the one next to it.

Oil trap
An underground rock structure that gathers and concentrates petroleum. Oil geologists spend much of their time looking for oil traps.

Oxbow lake
A curved lake formed from a *meander* in a river that has gradually been cut off by deposits of *sediment*.

Ozone layer
A layer in the Earth's atmosphere that is particularly rich in a type of oxygen called ozone. It is important to life on Earth, since it helps to filter out harmful rays from the sun. Pollution by industrial gases tends to break down the ozone layer.

P

Peninsula
A narrow piece of land that stretches into the sea or a large lake: an "almost island."

Permafrost
The phenomenon whereby a layer of frozen soil under ground does not thaw even during the summer. At high latitudes, this results in waterlogged landscapes, called *tundra,* where the meltwater from the surface cannot drain away.

Pingo
A landscape feature associated with *permafrost,* consisting of an underground "blister" of ice that expands and pushes up into a soil-covered mound. Pingoes can be up to 197 feet (60 m) high.

Plate tectonics
The movement of the Earth's surface as a series of plates, constantly being created at one side (in *ocean ridges*) and destroyed at the other (in *ocean trenches*). These plates are constantly moving, and cause earthquakes and mountain ranges where they collide.

R

Reef
A body of rock that lies just below the surface of the water. *Corals* can form reefs.

Rift valley
A valley formed as the Earth's crust stretches, and an area of land subsides between cracks or faults.

Rock cycle
The process whereby rocks are broken down by the force of *erosion,* the debris transported by rivers, *glaciers,* wind, sea currents, and so on. This debris is eventually deposited, buried, and turned into other rocks. In other parts of the process, rocks are heated and compressed in the depths of the Earth to become new rocks, or rocks are melted and resolidified into new rocks.

S

Sandbar
A deposit of sand, either underwater or just breaking the surface as a sandy island, formed by the movement of waves and sea currents.

Savanna
Dry tropical grassland with few trees. It borders the equatorial forests.

Schist
A *metamorphic rock* whose twisted shape and flattened *crystals* show the pressure under which it was formed.

Sediment
Loose rocky material eroded from the land and deposited on a seafloor, riverbed, or desert basin.

Sedimentary rock
A rock formed when *sediment* is laid down by the process of *erosion,* and then compressed, and the particles cemented together.

Shale
A fine-grained *sedimentary rock* formed by the solidification of mud.

Shield area
A region of ancient *metamorphic rocks* found in the heart of a *continent.* They are given individual names, such as the Canadian Shield and the Baltic Shield.

Soil
The mixture of broken rocky material and plant debris that forms the surface layer of the Earth.

Solstice
The time of the year when the sun is at its highest point or its lowest point in the sky.

Spring tide
The tidal condition that occurs twice a month when the gravitational influence of the sun and the moon are pulling in the same direction. During spring tides, there is a large tidal range, with the high tides being particularly high and the low tides particularly low. The opposite condition is the *neap tide.* The name is misleading, however, since the spring tide has nothing to do with the season of spring.

Strata
The layers in which sedimentary rocks form.

Subcontinent
An area of land that has the characteristics of a *continent* but is still attached to a larger landmass. India is an example.

Supercontinent
A very large continent, usually formed by the coming together of individual continents during the process of *plate tectonics.* A supercontinent may eventually break up into smaller ones, again by means of *plate tectonics.*

T

Tectonic
To do with the movement of the Earth's surface and the building of mountains.

Tombolo
An island that is attached to the land by a *sandbar.*

Trade winds
The prevailing winds that blow toward the *equator.* They are generated by the warm air rising over the hottest area of the Earth, and cooler air to the north and south sweeping in to take its place. They do not blow due north and south, but are deflected to the west because of the *Coriolis effect.*

Tundra
In the northern hemisphere, the northernmost icy plains covered with snow and ice thaw out during the brief summer. The soil at depth remains frozen, known as *permafrost,* so the meltwater on the surface cannot drain away. The result is a treeless landscape of lakes and marshes, known as tundra.

Typhoon
The local name for a hurricane in the Indian Ocean or China Sea.

U

UTC
Universal Time Coordinated. An internationally agreed basis for timekeeping, introduced in 1972 and based on International Atomic Time, by means of atomic clocks and satellites.

V

Volcano
The vent through which *lava* and *ejecta* are erupted during a *tectonic* upheaval. The material builds up around the vent to form a mountain, usually with a *crater* in the top. There are two kinds of volcano—broad, flat *basaltic volcanoes,* and steep-sided, conical *andesitic volcanoes.*

W

Water cycle
The constant movement of water from the oceans through evaporation into the atmosphere as vapor, onto the land as rain, and back to the oceans through the movement of rivers.

Index